We Must Change the Way We Live

PAT OBI

WE MUST CHANGE THE WAY WE LIVE

An Introspective View of the Value of Education and Financial Prudence in a Changing World

PAT OBI

Archway Publishing books may be ordered through booksellers or by contacting:

Archway Publishing
1663 Liberty Drive
Bloomington, IN 47403
www.archwaypublishing.com
1-(888)-242-5904

Because of the dynamic nature of the Internet, any web addresses or links contained in this book may have changed since publication and may no longer be valid. The views expressed in this work are solely those of the author and do not necessarily reflect the views of the publisher, and the publisher hereby disclaims any responsibility for them.

Any people depicted in stock imagery provided by Thinkstock are models, and such images are being used for illustrative purposes only.
Certain stock imagery © Thinkstock.

ISBN: 978-1-4808-0852-2 (sc)
ISBN: 978-1-4808-0853-9 (e)

Library of Congress Control Number: 2014910651

Printed in the United States of America.

Archway Publishing rev. date: 10/6/2014

To Megan

Contents

Acknowledgements

It is almost impossible for me to imagine the successful completion of this book without the help of Cheryl Nichols, Uche Onyebadi, Shomir Sil, and Jade Lee Lynch-Greenberg. Your suggestions for editorial and content improvements were invaluable. I remain in your debt.

The compilation of data for this project began in early 2009, as the global financial crisis was unfolding. Later that year, I had an opportunity to go on a study-abroad trip to China with my students in the MBA for Executives program at Purdue University Calumet. The various discussions we had, during that trip, about the impact of the crisis on America's global competiveness partly informed my views in this book. For that, I am grateful to the students. I am also grateful to Mayor Thomas McDermott, Jr. of Hammond, Indiana; Chancellor Thomas Keon of Purdue University Calumet; my colleagues in the College of Business; and the entire Purdue community for their support of my professional endeavors. I am forever grateful to the Board of Trustees of Purdue University who, on February 20, 2014, ratified my appointment to the high academic honor of an endowed professorship—White Lodging Professor of Finance.

A world of thanks to The Rev Michael Pfleger for his encouragement through the years. Friends and colleagues who have greatly inspired me and without whom the good story of this book could not have been told include Angel Vargas, Bradley Hassee, Calvin Richards, Casimir Barczyk, Charles Capek, Daniel Doyon, Daniel Gbedzeker-Williams, Dushan Nikolovski, Elvia Fuentes, Emuboh Gbagi, Enrique Mendez, Felicia Middlebrooks, Gregory Ash, He Li, Joshua Lybolt, Karen Bishop Morris, Kasia Firlej, Mahdee Iqbal, Marc-Anthony Doyon, Michael Preston, Mita Choudhury, Neeti Parashar, Odion Clunis, Regina

Biddings-Muro, Renate Schneider, Robert Lendi, Sebastien Zerbib, Wole Gansallo, and Wonga Hexana. Thanks to all of you!

My deepest gratitude to my beloved dad, mom, and siblings: Chiggy, Winnie, Austin, Ekeoma, Greg, Francis, and Felix. My dad, who lived to see me rise to the rank of full professor in academia, was, unfortunately, deceased before this project began. Together with my mother, he instilled in me the enduring values of hardwork and personal discipline, which I now seek to pass on to my beloved daughter, Megan, the best child there is.

A big thank-you to my publishers at Archway Publishing for their valued advice and guidance. Finally, to all who read this book, thank you for making the choice to seek the wisdom within it. I hope it enlightens you in the best of ways. Any deficiencies in the content and writing are of course mine. And for those, I apologize beforehand.

List of Tables

Preface

This book is about money and is written for a general audience. When we plan carefully and use money wisely, we are the better for it. When we ignore the prudence the use of money requires, we face problems that often lead to a life of misery and lack. With this in mind, this book shows how our choices regarding the use of money can be the difference between a life of financial hardship and a life that is financially secure.

There are three parts to this book, all of which ultimately deal with financial prudence. In the firm belief that knowledge is power and that a good education is the foundation for a secure financial life, I dedicate the first part to the overarching value of cutting-edge education. It addresses the question, how can we—both individually and as a nation—make the type of educational choices that can improve our chances of having a fulfilling career, as well as maintaining America's global competitive edge?

Part II deals with personal finance. I present easy-to-understand working models on how to prepare a financial plan, manage a budget, and invest for retirement. I also discuss how to make optimal choices concerning life insurance, estate planning, and personal debt. For many of us, debt is a major impediment to enjoying a fulfilling and peaceful life. It is also a major factor that can undermine our quality of life. For this reason, I devote the last chapter of this section to explaining the difference between, and the financial impact of, the so-called good debt and bad debt. I then show a path for eliminating overbearing debt.

The third and final part offers a national perspective on a key issue that threatens our economic strength and financial independence: excessive debt. Our national debt is excessive because, since 2011, how much we owe as a nation has exceeded our national output. I address this worrisome matter by pointing out, quite rigorously, that it will most definitely require financial sacrifices across the board to successfully tackle this problem.

When all parts of the arguments are connected, I conclude with a big picture that places service to others as the ultimate confirmation of our personal success. It is also, as I point out, the basis upon which the American nation is positioned to remain strong and competitive.

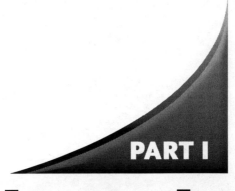

PART I

EDUCATION, EDUCATION, EDUCATION

Chapter 1. First, a Personal Story

A dream is your creative vision for your life in the future.

—*Denis Waitley*

In his 1931 book, *The Epic of America*, James Truslow Adams writes that the American dream is the dream of a people "in which life should be better and richer and fuller for everyone, with opportunity for each according to ability or achievement." This view of our national ethos captures the thrust of this book—self-empowerment. Since I first began my life in America in the mid 1980s, I have found that the realization of this dream is premised on three crucial factors: education, hard work, and financial prudence.

From time immemorial, education has been rightfully regarded as the singular factor that unlocks the myriad of opportunities that enable one to compete in the global sphere. The renown of civilizations past and present—Roman, Byzantine, Ottoman, and the epoch of Western civilization, among others—would not have been possible without the advances they made in science, technology, and leadership. In almost every society, the collective value and potential of educated people is reflected in how, individually, everyone contributes in building up the wealth and strength of the nation. Education is also the means by which one is able to help lift up others who are less fortunate. Without the benefits of the skillset that a good education provides, one is limited in his or her ability to be of service to others.

Needless to say, the value of a good education cannot be sustained without hard work and financial prudence. The American nation, from its inception, has exemplified strong work ethic and creativity by being at the forefront of some of the greatest inventions in modern science, such as the gas-powered automobile, the television, rocket science, electronics, appliances, the computer, and the Internet. These discoveries have made it possible for Americans to enjoy one of the highest standards of living in the world, which is the reason many people in and outside of the United States view America as the land of opportunity. Precisely for this reason also, millions of people from different corners of the globe have endured hardships and paid obscene amounts of money for a chance to study, work, and live in the United States. I happen to be one of them.

Unfortunately, some cynically view America as an empire whose time will someday come to an end, just like the empires in the past. I disagree with this assessment for three key reasons. First, unlike other powerful nations and empires, the United States is a nation of immigrants and a union of free-willing states and peoples. Second, the United States does not, and has never, coerced any other nation to become a part of it. Finally, while it remains a work in progress, the United States is a self-contained, self-sustaining, and vibrant democracy where personal liberties are written into its Bill of Rights.

As I see it, however, the real threat to the strength and stability of the American nation comes not from political excesses but rather from the combined effects of an underprepared, noncompetitive labor force and financial imprudence. Whereas the benefits of cutting-edge education can never be overemphasized, money remains the fuel that runs the engine of our free-market economy. For this reason, when prudence is lacking in the use of money, we face a debacle that could easily undo decades, if not centuries, of hard-won successes, as was hinted by the 2008 financial crisis. My concerns in this respect are informed by what I see as a dichotomy between recent trends in American life and what I have always cherished as the America of my dreams.

Growing up in the late 1960s and early 1970s in the war-ravaged southeastern Nigerian enclave once known as Biafra, I dreamed earnestly of living in a country where food, peace, and opportunities abound—in that order, actually. In my dreams, I saw America as one such place. Although I was little more than a toddler at the time, I remember how we starved and lived in great fear during most of the years of that horrendous civil war. Bombs fell everywhere we ran. Babies and children were often abandoned by their parents in the chaos. Many were killed. Many more died of starvation. Millions of children suffered from acute malnutrition and a severe form of protein deficiency called kwashior-kor. We lived mostly in the inner countryside, in our attempt to escape the onslaught of falling bombs from the incessant daily air raids of the Nigerian military.

The Nigerian Civil War was the result of a deep-running mistrust between the predominantly Islamic north and the mostly Christian south of the country. The Igbos make up the bulk of the ethnic communities of the southeast. Many liken the Igbos to the entrepreneurial prowess of the Jewish nation, by their exceptional advances in education, commerce, and, until that time, political leadership. Although the Igbos are the third largest ethnic group in Nigeria, following the Hausas and Yorubas, the first Nigerian president, after independence from Great Britain in 1960, was an Igbo named Nnamdi Azikiwe. However, Abubakir Tafawa Balewa, a northern Muslim, was the prime minister under Nigeria's parliamentary system of government. In 1966, a coup d'état led by a top Igbo military officer caused a sharp backlash against Igbos living in the north of the country. Thousands of Igbos were killed in a genocide that first brought the religious dichotomy of Nigeria to the fore. Some historians estimate the number of Igbos killed at more than a million.

There are many adults who remember very little of their early childhood. I am not one of them. Suffering and hunger made it impossible for me to forget my difficult childhood. During the Nigerian Civil War, we ate almost anything that had life in it—except human beings. On many occasions, we would go deep into the forest, scouting for nuts, rodents, and wild vegetables for food. Just about the only people who appeared well nourished at the time were Catholic priests, who on occasion would ration out cornmeal and dried milk, courtesy of Catholic Relief Services.

There were times my second elder sister and I would take turns accompanying my mother to a distant village market, ten miles away, just to sell a handful of vegetables grown in our little garden. We would then use the money to buy food. The last day I accompanied my mom to this market is a day I will never forget. As was always the case, we set out in the wee hours of the morning with our tiny produce—on foot, of course. Later in the evening, after we sold our merchandise and bought some food items with the proceeds from our sale, we set out again on the long trek home. On our way home, the heavens unleashed the heaviest thunderstorm I had ever seen. It was accompanied by a hailstorm with golf-ball-sized hail. I remember crying and saying to my mother that I had never suffered so much in my life. As I came to learn, that statement stuck with her for many years to come. She cried quietly, she later told me, the entire three agonizing hours it took us to walk back to where we camped.

In those very dark days of the war, we were forced by constant air raids to move from place to place. There were no proper schools in the places we took refuge. However, my parents made us go to some school whenever possible. There were makeshift schools in faraway villages and refugee camps. Classrooms were under the shade of big trees because most roofed buildings were already destroyed by constant bombardments. In any event, we could not risk staying in roofed buildings, as those were regular bombing targets. The teachers themselves were refugees. I think any adult who spoke proper English could volunteer to teach something, anything. We sang a lot of kiddie songs and prayed a lot, perhaps more than we learned. It was generally believed that death was imminent.

The dream of a peaceful world with enough to eat was so fleeting in those awful times that I thought of such a world as Utopia. Those were horrific times for any human being to live in. I shudder to think that millions of children in many parts of the world live these awful and harrowing experiences on a daily basis. The Nigerian Civil War eventually ended in 1970. My parents, by and large, regained their prewar employment, and our quality of life and standard of living improved thereafter.

By Nigerian standards, I grew up in a middle-class family. In 1966, my father graduated with a diploma in business administration from Waterloo Lutheran University (now called Wilfrid Laurier University) in Ontario, Canada. For many years, before and after the Nigerian Civil War, he was the personnel manager of a government-owned brewery in southeastern Nigeria. My mother was a schoolteacher. However, with a family of eight children, the family budget was very tight.

Education, above all else, was stressed in my family as if our next day's existence literally depended on it. My mother, especially, would take us to task if we failed to do our homework or, worse, received a bad report from school. On the flip side, we were profusely celebrated at the end of the school term, each time we brought home a good report. In our home, we did not swear, call each other names when angry, or talk back to Dad or Mom.

The pressure to be disciplined was particularly heavy on me, being the eldest male (the third child). I became an altar boy; I religiously (no pun intended) woke up in the early hours of each morning to serve at church and tutored my younger siblings in their homework. Later, in seventh grade, I was enrolled in a faraway Catholic boarding school, a type of junior seminary. My parents concluded it was a good environment to learn proper discipline as well as get a good education. I thought somewhat differently, though. From what I remembered of my hunger days during the Nigerian Civil War, Catholic priests lived well and ate well. Becoming one, I surmised, meant I could never go hungry if all hell were to break loose again.

Boarding schools used to be the norm in Nigeria, and it was not considered a privilege to go to one. It was also not viewed as an easy way to get rid of your children, as it is sometimes interpreted in the West. There were actually fewer day schools than boarding schools in Nigeria at that time. In a bid to impress my parents, I made sure not to spend all my allowance during the school term. Much to my parents' delight, I would return my unspent money when I came home for the holidays. I saved money in any way I knew. For example, to travel home during school break, I would stand by the highway in front of the school compound and flag down a freight truck rather than use regular public transportation. For this, I paid only a tiny fraction of what it would have cost me to take a taxi or a bus.

The unmatched parental love in our upbringing was demonstrated by the fact that my parents invested all they had in our education—all eight of us. They drove us to primary school every morning, visited us regularly in our boarding schools, and arrayed us in the finest wardrobe they could afford—so much so that we thought we were actually a rich family! The fact was, my parents owned no property, never really drove a decent car, and had absolutely no retirement savings. In their retirement years, however, they had a choice of living in one of eight comfortable homes—their children's homes.

It is easy to get the impression that my grammar school education, given the picture I have painted, was flawless. Nothing could be farther from the truth. I was expelled from the Catholic boarding school three years later for leaving the campus grounds without permission. I struggled through middle and high schools, although I always managed to do well enough to move up to the next grade. By the time I was ready for college, I was a veteran of three different boarding schools; but I graduated.

My initial desire upon going to college was to major in electrical engineering or some other discipline requiring quantitative skills. In Nigeria, such areas of study were generally considered lucrative when it came to employment and income. However, there was one problem: I was not good in mathematics coming out of high school. As a result, I settled for a general business major. I also wished to enroll in a university in Nigeria instead of overseas. At the time, it was often the case that the best and the brightest stayed back and studied in one of about four top universities in the country. For me, however, achieving a high enough score on the university entrance exam was a tall order. It was easier for me to settle, instead, for a four-year polytechnic in Nigeria, where I began diploma studies in general business.

For a number of reasons, the high opinion of the quality of post-secondary education in Nigeria began to wane in the early 1980s. It was also at this time that a series of terror attacks by an extremist Islamic group called *Maitatsine* erupted in the northern Nigerian city of Kano, where I was completing my national service. Fortunately, this was when I received the opportunity to continue my education in the United States. In 1984, I was admitted to the MBA program at Southwest Texas State University (renamed Texas State University in 2003).

Texas was full of challenges—educationally and financially. My four years of college in Nigeria were a cakewalk compared to the much more rigorous MBA curriculum at Southwest Texas State. On the financial side, my little savings from Nigeria, coupled with a good amount of help from my second sister, who had begun to work at that time, paid my tuition for my first semester of graduate studies. However, I did not have enough money to pay for living expenses, books, and other school supplies. All I possessed when I arrived in Texas was a small duffle bag containing a pair of pants, two T-shirts, an old plaid jacket given to me by my father, a photo album of my family, and a few items of hygiene.

Things got brighter a little later when I met a kind Nigerian student who introduced me to two money-saving opportunities. First, he took me to a thrift store on Congress Avenue in Austin. For less than ten dollars,

I left that store with much-needed clothing. Second, and more importantly, he connected me to six African students who shared a two-bedroom apartment in what I later learned was a run-down neighborhood in Austin's east side. I became the seventh roommate.

The Austin apartment was easily the best place I had ever lived. It might have been several weeks before I became conscious of the fact that it neither had proper plumbing nor running hot water. We boiled our water and took bucket baths. Nevertheless, I was very grateful for a number of reasons. First, I could afford to pay my share of the house bill, which came to thirty-eight dollars a month. Second, I had a place to lay my head—a tiny but big enough spot under an old dining table on the second floor of the apartment. Third, my roommates were kind enough to show me where to pick up odd jobs, which helped pay my bills as well as my school fees. At different times, I worked as a garbage man, a carpenter, a cook at a small fast-food kitchen, and a housekeeper for a group of physically disabled individuals (who were all in attendance as my family at my master's degree graduation).

Fortunately, I did not have to spend much money on food. Two of my roommates worked at the local Church's Chicken. At the end of their work shifts, they came home with plenty of leftovers. I carpooled to school in San Marcos, about thirty minutes south of Austin. By and large, I was able to save up enough money to buy my first car in early 1984—a 1980 Ford Fairmont with a white top and blue body. I remember feeling like I was on top of the world on that cold but sunny day in January when I paid $1,800 for it. In the few hours I was not studying or working, I delighted myself with washing and waxing it. Altogether, I lived in Texas for a year and a half, which was the time it took me to successfully complete my MBA studies at Southwest Texas State. I left for the University of Mississippi in late 1985 to begin my doctoral studies in finance.

I chose finance as my PhD major on the advice of Percy Poon, an MBA classmate and, in many ways, my mentor at Southwest Texas State. All through my undergraduate and master's degree studies, I had struggled with quantitative courses, especially mathematics, statistics, and finance. But whenever possible, I latched myself to fellow students who were skilled in these subjects. Percy was one of them. He was an international student from Hong Kong and was easily the most intelligent student in my MBA classes. He coached me in my weak areas and encouraged me to join him in applying for a doctoral program in finance. He explained that finance PhDs earned some of the highest salaries in business schools. That sold me! Percy later went on to Louisiana State University for his PhD at about the same time I left for Mississippi. Today, Percy, like me, is a professor of finance.

At the outset, Mississippi was a very scary place. Horror stories were told of how black people were mistreated in that State. Quite frankly, the University of Mississippi, more popularly referred to as Ole Miss, was my least favorite choice for my doctoral studies. But they promised me a graduate assistantship—a type of academic scholarship—if I did well in my first academic year. Moreover, of the ten schools to which I applied for my PhD, Ole Miss had the lowest tuition. It was simply for these two practical reasons that I decided on Ole Miss.

True to their word, I was awarded a graduate assistantship in my second year of studies at Ole Miss, though it was not a full assistantship. But, coupled with the five dollars an hour I earned from working in the university library, it was more than sufficient to pay for my tuition and other expenses. In the four and half years it took me to complete my PhD studies at the University of Mississippi, I pretty much did nothing but study. And, as was always my style, I made friends with individuals who were much smarter than me.

This smart-buddy approach to learning was particularly helpful to me at Ole Miss. For one thing, I was enrolled in a program that is widely considered the most quantitative in graduate business studies. The challenge was even more intense because my graduate adviser also signed me up for a secondary doctoral field called econometrics, a branch of applied mathematical statistics. This decision (of which I was not a part) shook me to the core. I readily reminded myself that the only undergraduate course in which I made a failing grade was statistics!

With all my disabling deficiencies, I truly had my work cut out for me. Only my dorm resident advisor, Ronnie Tatum, who later became the best friend I could ever have had in Mississippi, would remember the countless times I came back to my room crying like an abandoned baby because I did not understand what was taught in class. I thought about my family and how disappointed they would be if I got kicked out because of poor performance. My grief was almost overwhelming.

However, I persisted. I attribute my triumph over mathematics to three student tutors at the Ole Miss Learning Center. All three were graduate students in engineering. The complexity of the doctoral program, as I quickly discovered, belongs in a sphere that cannot easily be compared to any other level of learning. Notwithstanding, I found that the more I learned math, especially calculus, the more it intrigued me. By the end of my second semester in the PhD program, I became a calculus tutor myself. Teaching calculus significantly strengthened my overall aptitude in mathematics, as well as its various applications in the fields of statistics and finance.

Despite a number of challenges along the way, Mississippi turned out to be a good place for me. It was true that a little over two decades earlier in 1962, James Meredith, the first black to attend the University of Mississippi, suffered great indignity as he attempted to enroll in that university. It took the intervention of the National Guard to force Ole Miss to allow him onto the campus to attend classes. There is no question that the sacrifice made by Meredith, and others like him, paved the way for the likes of me to become proud alumni of Ole Miss today. When I completed my doctoral studies in the summer of 1989, after four and half years of study, I was the first black student to graduate from Ole Miss with a PhD in finance and econometrics. I was also the first among my cohort of seven doctoral students to graduate from the program. All but one of the other students in the cohort were Asians.

Throughout my studies, at both the undergraduate and graduate levels, I never really had a reason to take out an education loan. It was simply not an option. I lived frugally, which I agree is often a euphemism for being cheap. The truth was that I certainly did not like being a student; it was important for me to graduate quickly and begin to enjoy life.

I liken college to a medicine that you must take to get well. It does not taste good, but you need it to be healthy. The quicker you took it, the sooner you got it over with. I do not recall going to any parties when I lived in Texas or Mississippi. I simply did not have the money or, for that matter, the time to do so. I graduated early from all my academic programs, not because I was particularly smart—as I have made quite evident—but because I rushed through them. Prolonging my time in school would have cost me much more than I could actually afford. For almost my entire time in college and graduate school, I was self-sponsored, which made my early appointment to the faculty at Purdue University Calumet all the more gratifying.

My employment letter from Purdue came almost a full year before I graduated from Ole Miss. Perhaps my most surreal moment after I began my academic career as faculty was the day I received my first paycheck. To some it might be considered a normal experience. To me, however, a monthly income that was in the thousands, albeit at the low end, was mind-boggling. Overwhelmed with joy, I did what was—for me, anyway—natural. I fell to my knees and cried like a baby. It was, after all, fewer than twenty years earlier that I was a starving derelict fleeing from the bombardment of Nigerian air raids. My career in academia was in every way imaginable the fulfillment of a dream that only a few years before could have been compared to the building of castles in the air. The only other time I felt such a deep sense of gratitude was the day I was sworn in as a citizen of the United States.

My teaching, research, and consulting in the field of finance and applied statistics have proved more than a great reward for my personal ambitions. This is a field of learning in which I have discovered inordinate passion and professional satisfaction. The empowerment it has imbued in me is the reason for the many teaching and research excellence awards I have received over the years. It also accounts for the several consulting opportunities with which I have been privileged to be connected in more than fifty countries, spanning five continents. This realization of a life's dream underscores my belief in the greater American dream.

Stories, many more compelling than mine, are told and retold each day in many parts of this great nation. The magic of these stories is strengthened by the fact that although black people in 2008 accounted for only 13 percent of the US population, this is the first and only Western nation in history to elect an African American as president. This is why through the years I have often wondered why many Americans, especially blacks like me, have allowed themselves to give up in the hopelessness of inner city neighborhoods. I lived in such a place in Austin, Texas. I saw the challenges of inner city life. In those days, I remember I would often tell my best friend, Jara Beckum, that education was our only passport out of the social barriers of that horrid environment. Regretfully, Jara, like many of my other black companions at the time, chose a different path.

In the same manner of reflection, I have always found it a contradiction that although Americans work exceedingly hard and earn so much money, many of us are barely able to pay our bills. In America, we live in some of the biggest homes in the world, drive some of the largest vehicles on public highways, own more cars per family than elsewhere, and have possessions that overflow from the inner rooms to our multicar garages. Yet, the average American household carries more debt than is found in any other industrialized country. And, at the national level, we find that we now live in a country where our public debt has surpassed the size of our economy. These are worrisome facts.

I find that the combination of poor access to quality public education and excessive debt has proven to be the greatest threat to our economic strength and global preeminence. While access to good education is a daunting problem for many young people, especially those in inner cities, many Americans who make it through college do so with incalculable personal debt.

Today, the cost of college education is a close second to the cost of health care, both of which have continued to rise at several times the rate of inflation. It is unsettling that when the US housing market collapsed in 2007, total American household debt matched the size of the US economy, which at the time was estimated to be $14 trillion.

Going forward, my desire is to help create awareness of how to refocus our competencies in order to become self-sufficient and more competitive globally. The perspectives and guidance I share in this book are grounded on this premise and informed by my personal and professional experiences through the years.

Chapter 2. Industry Trends and Education Planning

The only thing more expensive than education is ignorance.

—*Benjamin Franklin*

Education and personal finance go hand in hand for two important reasons. The first reason is that more education often leads to higher income. The second is that a higher level of education, in any form, is more likely to lead to a greater awareness of financial prudence. In seeking a higher level of education, I believe it is essential for one to choose a field of learning that leads to a fulfilling career, regardless of how much income that career attracts. Equally, it is important to pursue the type of education—in whatever form—that provides the skillset that will make it easy to get and keep a job. In this chapter, I begin a discussion of what I hope will offer a practical insight on the value of advanced education and how to financially plan for it.

As the pace of globalization accelerates in the twenty-first century, the types of skills needed to compete both domestically and internationally are becoming more and more specialized. Globalization has not only led to the integration of financial markets around the world but also to the elimination of barriers to international transactions. With cheaper labor and abundant resources overseas, we must, in North America, upgrade our skills to remain strong and competitive. To address this need, many US industries increasingly seek technical and specialized skills both at the middle and upper levels. These emerging trends make it necessary to plan and advance our competencies in the areas where future jobs abound.

According to the Hudson Institute, a Washington, D.C. free-market think tank, the supply of skilled labor in the United States will not catch up to demand until 2050.[1] This fact was highlighted in a 2011 skills gap survey results published by the Manufacturing Institute. In it, 67 percent of respondents indicated a shortage of available, qualified workers with most expecting the shortage to grow even worse.[2] Earlier, in 2006, the American Society for Training & Development (ASTD) reported that the greatest skills gap existed primarily in the areas of mathematics, reading, writing, leadership, teamwork, technical, and professional skills.[3]

STEM schools, which focus on mathematics and science education, report that science and engineering jobs are growing 70 percent faster than other occupations.[4] These industry trends indicate where I believe our educational efforts ought to be particularly directed. In colleges and universities, fields of study such as applied science, engineering, business, and computer science offer some of the greatest employment and income opportunities in these high-tech, high-wage jobs of the future.

It is regrettable that we have yet to find ways to make the study of mathematics and science attractive to grade school students here at home. In 2013, the Organization for Economic Cooperation and Development (OECD) published the results of a comparative study of mathematics and science skills among fifteen-year-old students in more than sixty nations and school systems. The survey itself was conducted in 2012. In

---

1   "Manufacturing: An American Dream," U.S. Tech, Volume 24, Number 12, December 1, 2009

2   *2011 Skills Gap Report*, Manufacturing Institute, accessed May 13, 2014, www.themanufacturinginstitute.org/Research/Skills-Gap-in-Manufacturing/2011-Skills-Gap-Report/2011-Skills-Gap-Report.aspx.

3   *Bridging the Skills Gap: How the Skills Shortage Threatens Growth and Competitiveness and What to do About it*, Fall 2006, The American Society for Training & Development, accessed March 3, 2014, www.lifelonglearningaccounts.org/pdf/BridgingtheSkillsGap.pdf.

4   STEM is an acronym for science, technology, engineering and mathematics. *The STEM School Blog*, accessed July 22, 2012, www.stemschool.com/2009/04/what-is-stem-school.html.

mathematics, the United States ranked twenty-sixth. We fared just as poorly in science, with a rank of twenty-first.[5]

The consequence of all this is a short supply of American graduates in specialized careers. This has led to a gaping shortage of skilled labor in the more lucrative technical and professional fields. To overcome this deficit in recent years, we have had to import much of our needed technical labor under the H-1B visa program, which allows US employers to temporarily hire foreign workers in specialty occupations. Government regulation defines such occupations as engineering, mathematics, physical and social sciences, biotechnology, medicine and health, accounting, and business. Many of the beneficiaries of this special visa program are from South Asia, mostly India.

There is an even more unsettling problem about the shortage of Americans in these vital fields of learning. If you paid a visit to a good number of American universities, you might find that many, if not most, of the academics in the science, engineering, technology, accounting, and finance units, are non-Americans—or at least individuals not born in the United States. You might also find a significant number of international students in these academic disciplines.

Lest I am misunderstood, I value beyond measure the unparalleled opportunity and privilege that the American higher education system has created for many around the world. I am a beneficiary of it. And I guard this privilege jealously. I also value two key benefits that American universities enjoy owing to international student admissions. The first is that the rich and diverse American culture and great heritage are passed on to millions the world over. Foreign graduates of American universities are perhaps our greatest and best ambassadors. The second benefit is even more practical. International student enrollment is a prime source of revenue for American universities, especially the privately funded ones. All that said, for us to remain globally competitive as a nation, we must forcefully apply ourselves in fields requiring mathematics, science, and, yes, also English, which is the world's *lingua franca*.

For those who choose not to go to college, vocational schools offer a great alternative for acquiring midlevel technical skills that modern industry sorely needs. *CBS Evening News* reported on October 9, 2011,

5 *PISA 2012 Results*, accessed December 6, 2013, www.oecd.org/pisa/keyfindings/pisa-2012-results.htm.

that half of US manufacturers faced skilled labor shortages, especially automotive technicians; carpenters; electricians; heating, ventilation, and air-conditioning (HVAC) technicians; aviation mechanics; plumbers; pipefitters; welders; and precision tool technicians. It is noteworthy that skilled trades workers consistently top the list of the most difficult positions to fill in repeated surveys conducted by ManpowerGroup.[6]

In a study published in the August 2011 issue of the *Chicago Fed Letter*, it was reported that US manufacturers find it difficult to attract highly skilled workers. The study also found that educational attainment correlated strongly with personal income in both manufacturing and nonmanufacturing sectors.[7] In other words, the higher the level of one's education, the greater the expected income.

The takeaway from all this is that individuals seeking to be competitive should aim for higher education and, if possible, seek to be educated in a technically-oriented field, or at least in a field where one can acquire a specialized skill. There is one final note here though. While it is true that being trained in a specialized field may prove to be particularly moneymaking, it is, in my view, even more important to direct one's educational efforts toward an occupation that is not only rewarding but also fulfilling — making sure to fully understand the employment and income prospects of the chosen field of learning.

Saving for College

With little doubt to spare, education remains the greatest investment in human endeavor. But, like every other investment, the expected career benefits must exceed the financial cost for its value to be fully realized. Making adequate financial provisions for advanced education is as important as making the decision to go for it. As every business practitioner knows all too well, the first step in laying the groundwork for a successful venture is financial planning.

Financially speaking, planning for education is much easier than

---

6 *2012 Talent Shortage Survey*, ManpowerGroup, accessed November 1, 2013, www.manpowergroup.us/campaigns/talent-shortage-2012.

7 Lombardi, Britton, and William A. Testa, "Why Are Manufacturers Struggling to Hire High-Skilled Workers?" *Chicago Fed Letter* #289 (August 2011).

planning for a brick-and-mortar investment. But a great deal of the responsibility lies on parents and guardians, who must consider the various available options for saving for a child's education. While the child is yet very young, parents can set up an education giftrust, open an education IRA, or go for the more lucrative 529 college savings plan. Saving for college or vocational education has never been easier since Congress passed the 529 plan, a tax-advantaged education savings program.[8]

Most 529 education investments are held in a mutual fund. Contributions to, and income earned in, a 529 plan are tax free as long as the funds are used to pay for education-related expenses. The plan is also portable, meaning you can switch the beneficiary's name at any time. And if the child for whatever reason does not need the money any longer, you can get your money back, less taxes, of course.[9]

The following college savings example is in the style I use in many of my financial workshops. Here, I lay out an investment process that shows how to reduce and perhaps even eliminate the necessity for a college loan. It answers a simple question: How much should I put away, periodically, toward my dependent's future college education?

Consider a six-year-old. In twelve years, this child should be college-bound. Suppose you plan for the child to enroll in an in-state public college. In 2013, the College Board reported that the total annual cost of such a college was $18,391 (total cost includes tuition, fees, room, and board).[10] I round this up to $20,000 to also include books and supplies.

In recent years, the cost of college education has been rising, often, by more than the rate of inflation. Between 2008 and 2013, for instance, the College Board showed that the total cost of college education rose by almost 4 percent per year. This means that if you bump up $20,000 by 4 percent each year for twelve years, you will find that it would cost $32,021 to pay for this child's first year of college.

---

8   For more about this tax-free education investment program, visit www. savingforcollege.com.

9   It is important to speak with your financial advisor and go over published reports before making any investments. Also, please note that tax laws change from time to time.

10 Sandy Baum and Jennifer Ma, *Trends in College Pricing 2013*, (Trends in Higher Education Series, College Board).

You can calculate the annual cost for each of the remaining three years of college by continuing to raise the annual cost by 4 percent each year. By doing this, you will find that the total cost for this child to complete his or her studies within four years in an in-state public college twelve years from now will be almost $136,000. The table below summarizes these facts.

Table 2.1. How Much Should I Save for College?

Current annual college cost (public)	$20,000
Expected college cost inflation rate	4%
Years until child enrolls in college	12
Estimated total cost at time of enrollment, year 1	$32,021
Total college cost for year 2	$33,301
Total college cost for year 3	$34,634
Total college cost for year 4	$36,019
Savings goal at time of enrollment (sum of total cost for four years)	$135,975

For parents and guardians, this means a college savings plan should be set up today and then a series of monthly investments accumulating to at least $135,975 in twelve years should be worked out. The emphasis here is *at least* because it is better to save more than the estimated minimum, erring on the side of caution.

In determining the minimum savings goal, some financial advisors calculate the *present value* of the projected annual college costs. This amount is how much each future annual payment is worth in today's dollars. When you carry out this calculation, you will come up with a lower amount than what will actually be required in the future. No surprises here, since a dollar today is worth more than a dollar tomorrow. For example, five dollars in ten years may be *equivalent in value* to one dollar today. I do not consider this extended financial mathematics necessary, or even wise. The reason, again, is because you want to deliberately overestimate your college savings goal rather than risk not saving enough.

In the end, any future college loan that is taken out by this student would have to be the difference between the balance on the college savings account and the savings goal at the time of enrollment. For example, suppose the college savings account balance at the time of enrollment is $100,000. Then, given the college savings goal of $135,975, the amount to be borrowed should not exceed the difference of $35,975. In borrowing, only government-backed Perkins or Stafford loans are sensible. Such loans provide guaranteed low interest cost, deferred repayment until after graduation, and interest tax deduction.

There are three interrelated issues to be mindful of when applying this model. First, the annual college cost of $20,000 used in this example is based on the *average* cost for public colleges and universities as compiled by the College Board in 2013.[11] The actual cost could be higher or lower in a given state. Private universities typically cost more because they are not subsidized by taxpayer dollars. Community colleges generally cost less.

The second issue is the number of years until the child's initial college enrollment. Note that the fewer the number of years, the less the total cost, since the inflation effect would be less severe. The third and final point is that if the child spends more than four years in college, the total cost of education will be greater. This last point is particularly important because many college students now take longer than four years to graduate. In 2006, NPR made a startling revelation that the average public university student takes more than six years to graduate.[12]

One important reason it may take longer to graduate from college is if the student is enrolled in fewer hours because he or she works while in school. But this might actually prove to be a good financial decision. If the student uses part of the employment income to pay for college expenses and therefore reduces or even eliminates the need to borrow, then a healthy financial choice has been made. Thus, while prolonging time in college is generally not a smart idea, taking this route may help keep a student away from the burden of debt in the future. Moreover, if

---

11 In its 2013 *Trends in College Pricing*, the College Board reported that the average cost of full-time enrollment for the 2013–2014 school year was $18,391 for public four-year colleges. The comparable cost for private non-profit four-year colleges was $40,917. This cost includes tuition, fees, room, and board.

12 Silver, Mark, "How to Earn a Degree Without Going Broke," *NPR*, October 24, 2006, www.npr.org/templates/story/story.php?storyId=6376343.

a student's job has relevance to the college major, it could also be used to satisfy an internship requirement and therefore provide the student with the type of work experience that could be an asset in a future job search.

Before taking out a college loan, it is prudent to ensure that the expected future income from postcollege employment is sufficient to pay off the loan in a timely manner. This will help the student avoid the financial stress that comes from carrying an oversized loan or worse, an overdue education loan which, even while it is in deferment or forbearance, continues to accumulate interest. This hardship has the potential to further complicate future financial life, especially in the first few years of postcollege employment.

One important way to reduce the need for a college loan in the future is to work with a financial advisor to determine how much periodic contribution to make into the child's college savings. These periodic investments are designed such that their accumulated value—at the time the child goes to college—is at least equal to the expected total college cost. In the above college planning example, this amount is $135,975. To make this determination, there is one more variable that must be considered: the average percentage return one can expect to earn on the periodic investments. Financial advisors and, certainly, 529 education plan managers can offer suggestions in this regard, since many of these plans are designed to reflect the beneficiary's current age and the number of years until the funds will be used to pay for education expenses.

To show how this works, I offer a simple example, building on the college planning example shown above. Suppose that over the next twelve years, until the child enrolls in college, the college savings fund is expected to earn an average rate of return of 10 percent per year. This can be viewed as the annual 'interest rate' the fund will earn over the period. With the use of a financial calculator, the annual contribution is found to be $6,359. Dividing this annual figure by twelve gives the monthly contribution of $530.[13]

---

13 With a financial calculator, type in $135,975 as future value (FV), 12 as number of periods (N), 10 as the interest rate (I or r); then calculate annual payment (PMT) to get $530.

Table 2.2. How Much Should I Invest Monthly for College?

Savings goal	$135,975
Years until college enrollment	12
Average annual portfolio rate of return	10%
Calculated yearly investment amount	$6,359
Dividing the yearly amount by 12 gives the monthly investment	$530

To summarize, education savings goals should address the following three key factors: (1) the investment period, which is how long until the child enrolls in college; (2) college savings goal, which, in our college planning example, is determined to be $135,975; and (3) the rate of return that can be earned on the contributions until the child goes to college. In our example, 10 percent is the assumed annual rate of return.

Keep in mind that the result of this example is strictly based on the data used in the analysis. Each person's savings outcome will depend on the age of the beneficiary (the child), how many years until the child goes to college, and the expected investment rate of return. It is quite possible that the portfolio value at the time the child goes off to college may be less than how much is needed to pay for his or her education. Notwithstanding, the child is still a step ahead compared to where he or she would have been without a college savings plan. By carefully planning ahead, you help your dependent reduce, and possibly avoid, the need for a college loan.

What about College Loans?

College loans should be avoided as much as possible. They add to the financial burden that may already be in place owing to overdue consumer loans, such as those created by the use of credit cards. This is a persistent problem for many young American college graduates. According to CNN Money, about two-thirds of students graduating with four-year degrees in 2010 owed, on average, $23,186 in student loans.[14] For many college graduates, this loan amount is more than one half of their annual income in the first few years of employment.

Keep in mind, education loans, unlike consumer loans, are not dischargeable in personal bankruptcy. It is also important to know that Uncle Sam will pursue borrowers into their retirement years to collect on delinquent student loans. Unless the law is changed, a provision in the 2008 Farm Bill allows the federal government to offset or even withhold Social Security and disability payments to recipients with outstanding education loans—even if the debt has been outstanding for more than a decade.[15]

Unfortunately, bankruptcy filings by Americans with college education have been on the rise because often, employment conditions have not justified the size of the loan that was taken out in their college years. In September 2011, the Institute for Financial Literacy found that college graduates were the fastest-growing group of consumers filing for bankruptcy protection. This group included individuals earning up to $60,000 per year, which accounted for almost 14 percent of all bankruptcy filings. Not surprisingly, the survey also showed that individuals with only a high school education accounted for the largest percentage of bankruptcy filers.[16]

When a college fund is insufficient and when family and friends are unable to help with college expenses, it is prudent to search for grants and scholarships rather than hastily apply for education loans. It is advisable to begin the search for free money early in the senior year of high school. A free scholarship matching service like Fastweb.com is very helpful in this respect. FastWeb (Financial Aid Search through the Web) is the largest and most complete scholarship search on the Internet. It provides access to a searchable database of more than 400,000 private sector

---

14 Annalyn Censky, "Surging College Costs Price out Middle Class," *CNNMoney*, June 13, 2011; accessed on April 22, 2012, http://money.cnn.com/2011/06/13/news/economy/college_tuition_middle_class.

15 Ellen E. Schultz, "Defaulted Loans May Haunt Seniors," *The Wall Street Journal*, May 8, 2010; accessed on April 22, 2012, http://finance.yahoo.com/news/pf_article_109011.html.

16 Ylan Q. Mui, "Study: College Graduates Driving Increase in Bankruptcy Filings," *The Washington Post*, September 12, 2011.

scholarships, fellowships, and grants. The FastWeb database is updated daily, and the site will send email notifications of new scholarships that match a personal background profile.

Once enrolled in college, the first port of call should be the financial aid office. That is where a student can obtain all the information about financial assistance. When approval of the Free Application for Federal Student Aid (FAFSA) is granted, it is wise to accept only the grants and avoid the loans as much as possible.

While in college, working and living modestly remain an age-old way to be financially independent and therefore further reduce the need for an education loan. Early in my career as an academic, in the 1990s, I became friends with three students—Wole, Joe, and Duane—whose lifestyle closely resembled mine just a few short years before. They all worked full time while enrolled full time in the university. Wole lived with a couple of roommates in a small two-bedroom apartment not far from campus. Joe and Duane lived at home with their parents. Wole was a cab driver, Joe worked in a video rental shop, and Duane did construction work. It was obvious that there was little leisure time for them. But they all graduated *cum laude* with their bachelor's degrees within four years. And they did so without a penny of college loans! From their employment income, they were able to pay their fees as well as their modest living expenses. Personal and education expenses were minimal because of their lifestyle choices. I remember that Duane, in addition to paying his way through college, also paid rent at his parents' home. Today, all three of these individuals have executive positions in their places of employment; two are vice presidents in Fortune 500 firms. And so, while it may be true that the cost of college education has risen faster than personal income in recent years, working while in college remains a wise way to supplement other sources of funding.

Is College for Everyone?

Some like to say that college is not for everyone.[17] I am not so sure I necessarily agree with this point of view. In my opinion, college should not be viewed as a career, which may be suited for some and not for others. Postsecondary education, in general, ought to be viewed as a pathway to acquire the type of basic education that can position someone for a meaningful career and a living wage. Even more importantly, advanced education empowers one mentally. For many, it offers an unparalleled opportunity to compete in more spheres of life than would otherwise be the case.

The knowledge acquired from being educated endures. For this reason, at least, it is wise for everyone to aspire for a postsecondary education of some sort. The quest for knowledge is as basic a human need as any other basic conveniences sought in life. If one needs a place to live, does the person say "not everybody needs a home"? If one needs to provide for family, does the person say, "not everybody needs to work"? Yet, in each of these cases, education lays the groundwork that enables, or at least facilitates, the fulfillment of our basic needs for shelter and security.

It is sometimes said that you do not need education to be successful. I guess it depends on what is really meant by "successful." I remember back in the late 1990s there was this witty radio talk show host named Adam Carolla. In spite of his apparent goofiness, Mr. Carolla said some of the most intriguing things on his radio show, *Loveline*, cohosted by a psychiatrist, Dr. Drew Pinsky. In response to a caller's question one evening, Carolla explained, in his inimitable way, that he did not think you could consider yourself successful in an overall sense. Rather, you were successful only with regard to the completion of a specific task, after which you moved on to the next challenge. In other words, the journey to success never ends.

I liken Mr. Carolla's take on success to the following quote credited

---

17 A parallel argument is whether college is worth the money paid for it. This argument, addressed by Guy Lambert (Basic PLUS Level Expert author), makes the case—supported in this book—that the value of college education should be measured by job availability and income: Guy Lambert, "Is College Worth The Money Today?" accessed May 24, 2012, http://ezinearticles.com/?Is-College-Worth-The-Money-Today?&id=6825670.

to Benjamin Franklin: "Without continual growth and progress, such words as improvement, achievement, and success have no meaning." In effect, one does not quit at some point and then say "I am done." Arguing that one does not need to be educated to be successful is neither here nor there. If by being educated, the opportunity is created to obtain, or reinforce, the skills and aptitudes that can help one to become accomplished, then I daresay there is every reason to see a great benefit in the pursuit of advanced learning.

It is unfortunate that rather than seeing the big picture in being educated, some of us see the acquisition of much money as the epitome of success. If the quest for money precedes the desire to gain knowledge, then I fear the cart has been placed in front of the horse. As I see it, money never creates wealth; only brains do. If simply having a lot of money is the way a society becomes wealthy and self-sufficient, then all the oil-rich sub-Saharan African and Middle Eastern countries would be in the G-20 (the group of twenty most industrialized economies). Yet, these countries look to the West and the Far East to provide them with the technical expertise they need to run their economies.

On the flip side, a number of countries and territories have created an incredible amount of wealth for their citizens by massively educating their people. Such places as Denmark, Finland, Hong Kong, Japan, Netherlands, Singapore, South Korea, Sweden, and Switzerland are good examples. With virtually no natural resources of note, these countries have successfully turned their citizens to some of the wealthiest in the world while also boasting a much more equitable distribution of income than most other advanced economies.

At the end of the day, money is only a medium of exchange and has no value except in what it can buy. You can carry a basket full of cash, as was the case in most of the years that Robert Mugabe was the president of Zimbabwe, but it will do no good if it cannot buy a thing. Ultimately, the value that money possesses depends on the resources an educated human mind can skillfully put together to help improve the quality of life for all.

Chapter 3. Education versus Income

The best education in the world is that got by struggling to get a living.

—*Wendell Phillips*

Knowledge remains the greatest asset with which to compete in our increasingly specialized global economy. More than ever, we are in a knowledge economy where the reward from any employment goes with the skillsets the employee brings to the workplace. The opportunity to earn a decent income is increasingly difficult for those lacking basic education.

As our modern economy becomes more and more specialized, basic education has gradually moved up from high school to college. Individuals with less than college education are forced to compete for fewer jobs at the low end of the job market. And even then, many have to work two or three of these jobs to keep pace with the rising cost of living. Also important is that in the global job market, one is up against millions in the developing regions of the world who, for the same type of job, would happily accept pennies on a dollar for a day's wage.

Back in 2009, the National Governors Association projected that by 2014, almost 75 percent of future jobs would require employees to possess a post-high-school education or at least a license or certificate. Their report eloquently concludes that higher education is necessary for one to compete more effectively in tomorrow's job market. Occupations requiring a bachelor's degree are projected to grow the fastest, nearly twice as fast as the national average for all occupations. More importantly, the report showed that the earnings advantage of a college education has widened considerably in recent years. Someone with a bachelor's degree can expect to earn 75 percent more than a high school graduate over a lifetime.[18]

Is the Cost of Higher Education Worth it?

As the challenges of getting a job intensified through the late 2000s—a consequence of the Great Recession that began in 2008 and lasted for upward of five years—some pundits questioned whether the high cost of college education was justified.[19] This is a well-founded concern. However, this is a concern that needs to be considered in context. No one expects a bad economy to last forever. Therefore, the difficulties college graduates typically experience in the wake of any recession should not be viewed as a condition of permanence.

In any event, the alternative (not having a college education) is much worse. If getting a job with a college education is difficult, try looking for a job in a bad economy without one. The odds of getting a job under such conditions, and one that can pay a living wage, are undoubtedly much tougher. I dedicate a great deal of this chapter to demonstrating these facts. I also spend a good amount of time showing the employment and income facts for various college-based careers as well as a path for planning and saving for higher education.

Many young people hang their entire hopes on sports and show business. I love sports, and I also love showbiz. But I would be deceiving any young man or woman if I encouraged him or her to solely pursue a career that is not based on formal education. The odds of success in these fields are known to be few and far between. Arguably, there is a place for sports and show business in the cultural evolution of a society.

---

18 David Wakelyn, "Increasing College Success: A Road Map for Governors," NGA Center for Best Practices, December 9, 2009, accessed December 20, 2010, www.nga.org/files/live/sites/NGA/files/pdf/0912INCREASINGCOL-LEGESUCCESS.PDF.

19 See, for example the following article: Guy Lambert (Basic PLUS Level Expert author), "Is College Worth The Money Today?", accessed May 24, 2012, http://ezinearticles.com/?Is-College-Worth-The-Money-Today?&id=6825670.

Ultimately, however, it is the advances in science, management, and liberal arts that drive society to the next level of innovation and civilization. With all their physical prowess and sports genius—for which the likes of Astylos of Crotona, Leonidas of Rhodes, and Polydamas of Skotoussa were famed—what really made ancient Greece the great nation it once was were the contributions to learning by the likes of Archimedes, Euclid, and Pythagoras. It is noteworthy that while Pythagoras was a renowned boxing champion, what he is solely known for today are his contributions in mathematics.

Arthur Ashe, who passed away in February 1993, was the first African-American to win the US Open, Australian Open, and Wimbledon. He scored many other firsts in his career and was eventually elected to the Tennis Hall of Fame in 1985. But one thing for which I will always remember this great man was what he said in a TV interview sometime in the late 1980s, perhaps early 1990s, after winning one of his numerous tournaments. The question was how he felt about being viewed as a hero. In response, he said he was no hero; he did not save anybody. He said athletics was something one did for oneself and in the process, entertained people. It should, therefore, never be the basis for considering the value of an individual to society. More importantly, he added that the story would be different if he were to have done or discovered something that benefited society, such as finding the cure for cystic fibrosis (my first time of learning about this disease). I could not agree more with Mr. Ashe.

As mundane as it might sound, more education offers greater employment opportunities, as well as better job security. At the height of the Great Recession that followed the 2008 Global Financial Crisis, employment data from the Bureau of Labor Statistics (BLS) showed that in 2010, the average monthly unemployment rate for college graduates was 4.7 percent, less than half the jobless rate for those with only a high school diploma. It was much worse for those with less than a high school diploma—a staggering 15 percent. As the following table shows, the employment advantage of college graduates over nongraduates is a long-term trend.

Table 3.1. Average Unemployment
Rate by Level of Education⁺

Year	Less than High School	High School, No College	Some College, Associate Degree	Bachelor or Higher
2003	8.8	5.5	4.8	3.1
2004	8.5	5.0	4.2	2.7
2005	7.6	4.7	3.9	2.3
2006	6.8	4.3	3.6	2.0
2007	7.1	4.4	3.6	2.0
2008	9.0	5.7	4.6	2.6
2009	14.7	9.8	8.0	4.6
2010	14.9	10.3	8.4	4.7
2011	14.1	9.4	8.0	4.3
2012	12.4	8.3	7.1	4.0
2013	10.9	7.5	6.4	3.7

+ Based on the monthly unemployment rates for each category as published in the *Labor Force Statistics from the Current Population Survey*, US Bureau of Labor Statistics, accessed on May 15, 2014, http://data.bls.gov/cgi-bin/surveymost?ln. Data are for individuals 25 years and over.

There is a curious pattern in the jobless rate when broken down by level of education and ethnicity. As many already know or suspect, unemployment rate for all levels of education is highest for blacks, followed by Hispanics. As the following BLS data for 2012 show, unemployment rate for blacks, in many cases, was almost twice that for whites. These two demographic groups show the widest variation in the jobless rate. This is also a recurring pattern for all the years such data have been compiled by the BLS.

Table 3.2. 2012 Unemployment Rate by Ethnicity

Level of Education	White	Black	Asian	Hispanic
Bachelor's degree and higher	3.7	6.3	4.3	5.1
Associate's degree	5.4	10.2	6.3	8.0
Some college	6.9	11.6	7.0	8.0
High school graduates	7.5	13.4	6.1	9.0
Less than high school	11.4	20.4	6.8	11.0

Data source: *Labor Force Statistics from the Current Population Survey*, US Bureau of Labor Statistics, accessed on May 15, 2014, www.bls.gov/cps/cpsaat07.htm. Data are for individuals 25 years and over.

Some pundits might argue that this is yet more evidence of unfair discrimination in the US labor market. However, a fact that should also not be lost on anyone is that if you are black or Hispanic, you have an even greater reason to seek advanced learning—to minimize your chances of unemployment. If you are disadvantaged on various grounds, what you should do is to aspire to rise to a level where your disadvantages are at a minimum, making sure that you not allow yourself any excuses for failure. In my view, if for any reason you are disadvantaged and you throw in the towel as a result, then you have only raised your disadvantage level twofold.

Going a step further, there is no doubt that education pays and that it pays with higher income and greater employment opportunities. In its *Current Population Survey* for 2013, the Bureau of Labor Statistics showed that the median weekly earnings for individuals with bachelor's degrees were $1,108 while those with high school diplomas were only $651.[20] The numbers get much smaller for those without high school education. Americans with less than high school education are disadvantaged on two fronts. First, they suffer the highest unemployment rate. Second, even when employed, they earn the lowest income.

---

20 *Current Population Survey*, U.S. Department of Labor, U.S. Bureau of Labor Statistics, accessed May 16, 2014, www.bls.gov/emp/ep_table_001.htm.

Table 3.3. 2013 Earnings and Unemployment Rates by Educational Attainment

Education attained	Unemployment Rate (%)	Median Weekly Earnings
Doctoral degree	2.2	$1,623
Professional degree	2.3	1,714
Master's degree	3.4	1,329
Bachelor's degree	4.0	1,108
Associate's degree	5.4	777
Some college, no degree	7.0	727
High school diploma	7.5	651
Less than a high school diploma	11.0	472

Data source: *Current Population Survey*, U.S. Department of Labor, U.S. Bureau of Labor Statistics, accessed May 16, 2014, www.bls.gov/emp/ep_table_001.htm.

To be competitive in the job market—both at home and abroad—the basic education goal every American should aspire to is college level. In addition to the income and employment benefits, a college education is also where the foundation is laid for various cognitive attributes in our personal and professional lives. These include self-confidence, self-empowerment, improved aptitude, critical thinking and analytical skills, better communication skills, and better people skills. These attributes open doors to professional advancement in business, industry, and the professions. It is perhaps for these reasons that individuals with higher levels of education find it easier to get jobs and earn more money than those who are not college prepared.

Notwithstanding, it is fair to ask whether the ever-rising cost of advanced education is really worth it. Why spend all that money going to college when the expected monetary payoff may not be sufficient to justify the cost? This is an important question that many cynics have raised on the airwaves, especially in the face of the escalating cost of college education and the occasional weak job market.

Later in this chapter, I offer what I believe to be a practical approach to planning for college. But first, let me hasten to point out that it is ironic that none of the college education cynics known to appear on the TV chatter are without a college education. In fact, the reason they have jobs on the airwaves is, in all likelihood, because they are college educated. I have yet to hear any of them say "I wish I never went to college." Notwithstanding, the question as to whether the cost of college education is justified by the expected benefits is an important one. So I will try to offer a context within which to examine and perhaps resolve this apparent disconnect.

In my view, when it comes to deciding on college education, there are two interrelated issues that should first be reconciled. The first is that college should be viewed strictly as a conduit for graduating into a career. Going to college just to go to college may not, in and of itself, be a smart thing to do. The second, and perhaps more important, issue is that the career sought must be fulfilling. To be fulfilling, the career should meet three practical criteria: First, it has to lead to a job that can put food on the table. Second, the career must be one that makes one proud to practice it. And third, the individual must have the capacity to do well in the course of study leading into that career. The last point is especially important because it would be disheartening to get stuck in college while attempting to complete, and pay for, a program that is disproportionately difficult and/or unsuited to one's particular talents.

Choosing the Right College

If college is to be viewed as a conduit to a career, then it is prudent to consider the cost of the college to be attended. It is unwise to think, as some students do, that the quality of one's postcollege life will be defined by the name of the institution on the diploma. If you were asked to name the alma maters of the last ten US presidents, I bet you would be hard-pressed to name half of them. Likewise, I doubt that the best among us knows or remembers the universities attended by the most recent Nobel Laureates in any field. The point is, the name of the college or university is not as important as one's field of learning and certainly not nearly as important as the talent or skillset required in the workplace.

It is equally unwise to begin one's college experience by first choosing some expensive private college and then rushing to take out a large education loan to pay for it. This is a mistake that many students make, and one that is likely to have severe financial consequences in the years to come. The prudent thing to do, I believe, is first figure out how much money is available in one's college savings and then look for an affordable college. For some, a wise decision may be to get started at a community college and then work on completing the freshman and sophomore college credits there before proceeding to a four-year college.

If there is any factor worth considering when evaluating colleges, outside the cost, it is the graduation rate of its students. A graduation rate is the percentage of an incoming college class that graduates within six years of initial enrollment. Colleges with high graduation rates are viewed favorably by rating agencies. Notwithstanding, this information should be viewed with great caution since a variety of factors, many beyond the institution's control, play into the calculation. One such factor is the socioeconomic background of the majority of students in that college. Therefore, much more than information about the college itself, it is one's personal dedication to excel that ultimately determines a successful college experience.

Financing the Cost of Higher Education

If education savings is insufficient to pay for the chosen college, deciding how much in college loans to take out for the difference should be determined based on the *value* of one's future career. To elaborate, consider the college choices made by two hypothetical college-bound students: Mary and Jason. Both have decided on in-state colleges with a total cost of $20,000 per year. This cost is expected to increase over the next four years at four percent per year.[21] But here is the kicker: Mary is an electrical engineering major while Jason is a political science major.

The research firm, PayScale, publishes salary data by degree and major subject area of study. The data are reported in a range from the tenth to the ninetieth percentile. If your salary is in the tenth percentile,

---

21 Between 2008 and 2013, the College Board reported that the total cost of public four-year in-state colleges rose by approximately 4 percent per year. Total cost includes tuition, fees, room, and board (Sandy Baum and Jennifer Ma, *Trends in College Pricing 2013*, Trends in Higher Education Series, College Board).

it means that 10 percent of all published salaries are less than yours. Similarly, if your pay is in the ninetieth percentile, you make more money than 90 percent of the pack; you are almost at the top of the food chain, as it were. The published tenth and ninetieth percentile salaries for electrical engineers, updated on May 10, 2014, were $57,528 and $136,152, respectively. The corresponding data for individuals with a degree in political science were $34,386 and $109,688.[22]

PayScale's salary report shows clearly that regardless of the percentile, salaries for individuals with a degree in the analytical fields of business and engineering are, on average, higher than those with a degree in the liberal arts. The point here is not to say that one major field is better than the other. Far from it. It is, instead, the connection of field of learning to income expectation and the cost of financing one's education that is the focus. When Mary and Jason graduate with their bachelor's degree, they can expect their salaries to be at the low end of the percentile range in the first couple of years—about $57,000 for Mary, whose major is electrical engineering, and $34,000 for Jason with a major in political science.

We assume that Mary and Jason are good students, are enrolled full-time, and will graduate in four years. Suppose both decide to take out a college loan equal to 90 percent of the total cost of their education. This means that for the first year in college when the total cost is projected to be $20,000, the loan amount would be $18,000 for each student (see table below). Given the expected 4 percent annual increase in college costs, the annual cost for each of the college years is determined as shown in the table. For each of these projected costs, the amount to be borrowed—which, again, is 90 percent of the total cost of education—is also shown. With these calculations, we find that the total amount owed when these two fine students graduate from college will be in the neighborhood of $76,436 each.

---

22 *Average Salary by Degree/Major Subject for Country: United States*, Updated May 10, 2014, PayScale, accessed May 16, 2014, www.payscale.com/research/US/Country=United_States/Salary/by_Degree.

Table 3.4. Calculating the Total Cost of Financing Higher Education

Year	Total Cost (assuming 4% inflation rate)	Loan Amount (assuming 90% of cost of education)
Freshman	$20,000	$18,000
Sophomore	$20,800	$18,720
Junior	$21,632	$19,469
Senior	$22,497	$20,248
Total loan amount		$76,436

So here is the loaded question facing our two students: Will they earn enough during their early years of employment to pay off their loans as well as take care of their normal living expenses? This important question should precede the decision of whether or not to take out an education loan, and if so, what size of loan to take out.

In many cases, if not in every case, college loans are amortized and paid off in equal installments. By this financial arrangement, each monthly payment consists of a portion of the principal plus interest payable on the loan balance at the beginning of that month. In the case of Mary and Jason, let us assume that they have ten years to pay off their loans after they graduate. Also, let us assume an interest rate of 5 percent per year. Based on these figures, the calculated monthly loan payment would be about $811.[23]

Next, we line up this financial obligation with the monthly income out of which the payment will be made. To do this, we shall assume that our role-players, when employed, will take home sixty cents of every dollar they earn. The rest of their salary goes to pay for federal, state, Social Security, and local taxes as well as their share of employment benefits, such as 401(k) and health insurance. Based on these assumptions, the take-home monthly income for Jason would be about $1,700, which as you can see from the table below is a good $1,150 less than Mary's.

---

23 With a financial calculator, your input data are as follows: $76,436 is present value (PV); 120 is number of months (N); 5%/12 is interest rate—typed in as monthly rate. By computing the payment (PMT), your result is $811.

In case you wonder, the assumptions made in this analysis reflect the actual incomes found in the surveys presented earlier. It is also realistic to assume that about 40 percent of your top line income (gross income) would go toward taxes and benefits. The financial story for Mary and Jason is summarized as follows:

Table 3.5. Calculating Education Loan Payment and Residual Income+

	Mary	Jason
Total amount borrowed	$76,436	$76,436
Loan maturity (years)	10	10
Loan maturity (months)	120	120
Interest rate—annual	5%	5%
Monthly loan payment—calculated	$811	$811
Expected first year salary (tenth percentile)	$57,000	$34,000
Take-home monthly income (60% of gross)	$2,850	$1,700
Loan payment-to-income ratio	0.28	0.48
Loan amount-to-income ratio	1.34	2.25
Leftover income after monthly loan payment	$2,039	$889

+ To calculate loan payment, the use of a financial calculator is helpful. The input data are as follows: $76,436 is present value (PV); 120 is number of months (N); 5%/12 is interest rate, typed in as a monthly rate. By computing the payment (PMT), the result is $811.

As can be seen, almost half of Jason's take-home income goes toward loan payoff. For Mary, however, it is only less than a third. At this time, both of these individuals will also have to contend with various living expenses, including rent, out-of-pocket health care, food, transportation, telephone, and perhaps consumer credit card charges. Jason's financial situation is trickier because after each loan payment, he has only less than $900 left to pay for living expenses.

This analysis puts in full view the classic financial problem faced by many loan-laden college graduates. To ignore expected employment income when taking out a college loan is unwise. The danger for Jason is that while he borrowed as much as Mary, his subsequent capacity to pay off his loan after graduation is not nearly as strong as Mary's, who opted for a higher-income field of study. The important takeaway here, therefore, is that one's expected income should inform the decision of the size of the education loan.

I have neither attempted to suggest, nor have I indicated, that one's expected income should solely guide the decision of a college major or future career. Far from it. There is no discounting the fact that one's aptitude, likes, and abilities are some of the important drivers in the choice of a career and, therefore, a field of learning. The intent here is to reconcile the financing cost of advanced education with one's capacity to pay off the debt after graduation. While a college loan should be viewed as an investment, as some financial advisors rightfully argue, it is important to note that an investment's expected benefit has to outweigh the cost in order for that investment to be valuable. It is in this context that the value of any advanced education ought to be examined when it comes to how it should be financed.

Finally, it is wise for a college-bound individual to accept the fact that he or she may not in fact be able to afford the cost of his or her preferred college. Selecting an affordable college and then choosing a major that leads to a fulfilling career is a wise path to tread. If I were a prospective college student, this would be my mantra as I plan for a successful college experience. There is no pride or value in choosing a big name university and then dropping out later because either the cost has become overbearing or because the field of study, for whatever reason, has become too taxing.

Again, keep in mind that the basis for the above analysis is not to judge one college major over another. It is, instead, the financial practicality associated with paying for the education that is being assessed. To ignore it is to expose oneself to a possible financial danger after graduation.

Chapter 4: A Paradigm Shift for Public Education

If you are planning for a year, sow rice; if you are planning for a decade, plant trees; if you are planning for a lifetime, educate people.

—*Chinese proverb*

To go to college and succeed, a good high school education must first be in place. The quality of students that will fill our colleges and universities in the future will depend on how well the students were prepared in grade school. Even more important, the economic strength of the country will ever remain challenged if a significant number of us are undereducated.

Unfortunately, much is left to be desired about the quality of education in many of our elementary and secondary schools, especially those in the inner cities. Many efforts have been made over the years—at both the federal and local levels—to reform public education. Most notable were President George W. Bush's 2002 No Child Left Behind and President Barrack Obama's 2009 Race to the Top. The former law required states to give students in grades 3–8 an annual test in reading and mathematics. Among other things, Race to the Top would reward states for implementing performance-based standards for teachers and principals. Unfortunately, reforms such as these have yet to produce the intended result, which is to raise the proficiency level of high school graduates. Some critics attribute their failure to what they consider the self-serving agenda of teachers unions, education administrators, and legislators who often succumb to the whims of organized labor. My take on this is far less complicated.

I believe that the ever-widening gap between the rich and the poor in the United States can be explained, in large part, by the poor quality of education in our public schools. If students are poorly educated and, as a result, lack the skills to compete, they will be unable to secure the type of employment that can offer them a meaningful living wage. To be clear, education at the university level in the United States remains top-notch. This is because our postsecondary education is firmly rooted in innovation and discovery. And, it provides an incentive system that rewards the academic faculty for greater efforts. The crying shame, however, is the deplorable state of our elementary and secondary schools, the result of which is the huge gap between the competency level of many high school graduates and the aptitude level required of college freshmen.

The Challenges in Minority Communities

The failure of public education is particularly visible in the minority communities, where school dropout rates are high and where young people are often vulnerable to gangs, criminal activities, and substance abuse. In 2009, the Alliance for Excellent Education reported that nationwide, only 69 percent of high school students manage to graduate in four years. Even worse, only 55 percent of Hispanics, 51 percent of blacks, and 50 percent of Native Americans successfully complete high school in four years. In contrast, 76 percent of whites and 79 percent of Asian Americans graduate with a high school diploma over the same period.[24]

There is a lasting negative consequence of dropping out of high school both to the individual and the country at large. As I have shown elsewhere in this book, individuals with less than high school education earn significantly less than those with high school diplomas. They also face a greater employment difficulty. For the nation, there is a loss of productivity when a good chunk of the labor force is underskilled. In the report already cited, the authors of "Alliance for Excellent Education" found that 1.2 million high school students who would have graduated with the class of 2008 dropped out. These individuals, it is estimated, will end up costing the United States $319 billion in lost income over the course of their lifetimes.

Reports also show that poor high school performance often leads to low

---

24 "Understanding High School Graduation Rates in the United States," Alliance for Excellent Education, July, 2009, accessed May 16, 2014, http://all4ed.org/wp-content/uploads/2013/09/National_wc.pdf.

educational achievement at the college level. In 2008, for example, only 26 percent of blacks ages 25–37 had associate's degrees, compared to 38 percent for all populations in that age group. The outcome is worse for Hispanics; only 18 percent of Latinos in the same age group obtained two-year college diplomas.[25] Low educational attainment also tracks poverty. For example, census data for 2010, summarized by the National Poverty Center, showed that 27 percent of blacks and 27 percent of Hispanics were poor. In contrast, only 10 percent of whites and 12 percent of Asians were considered poor.[26]

The problem of low educational attainment for Hispanics may be more complex than for other minority groups. It is likely that the influx of Hispanic immigrants with low levels of education in recent years has added to the socioeconomic challenges of this demographic group. Many, like the former governor of California, Arnold Schwarzenegger, have argued that the poor English language skills of many Hispanics limit their employment opportunities and career advancement in the United States. Their plight has not been made easier by the accommodations that cities like Los Angeles, Miami, New York, and San Antonio make for Spanish speakers.

In 2011, a friend visiting New York City from South Korea for the first time expressed wonder at how both English and Spanish are often displayed side by side on many public notices. In some states, like Indiana, you can actually take your driver's license test in Spanish. With such accommodations, there is little incentive for a Spanish-only speaker to learn English and merge into the larger American society. It also unwittingly creates two parallel societies in the United States based on language. I believe this manner of accommodation to be a grave mistake. I think policy makers who think this is a good idea should take a trip to countries like Belgium, Spain, Cameroon, and, yes, also Canada to learn how linguistic differences often translate into social dichotomy and separatist sentiments.[27]

25 Ryu, Mikyung, *Minorities in Higher Education: Twenty-fourth Annual Status Report* (Washington, DC : American Council on Education, 2010).

26 "Poverty in the United States: Frequently Asked Questions," National Poverty Center, The University of Michigan, accessed July 23, 2012, www.npc.umich.edu/poverty.

27 The institution of Mandarin as the sole official language in China, following the 1949 Communist revolution, was strategic. Communist leader Mao Tze Dong considered it an important way to unify the fifty-nine Chinese nationalities after centuries of civil wars and foreign occupations.

There are more socioeconomic statistics that provoke additional thought about where the country is headed. Population projections for 2000–2050 by the Bureau of the Census show that the US population is expected to rise by an additional 184 million. Of this increase, Hispanics alone would make up 67 percent. Blacks will chip in an additional 14 percent.[28] These projections raise concerns for two important reasons. First, the direct correlation between poverty and low educational attainment suggests that if the current trend continues, the income gap might become even wider in the future than it is currently. Second and perhaps more worrying, since urban crime is more prevalent in the low-income minority communities, crime prevention may be a more challenging undertaking in the years to come.

At the Future of State Universities Conference held in October 2011, Steve Murdock, professor of sociology at Rice University and former director of the US Bureau of the Census, showed that in 2010, 38 percent of Hispanics had less than high school education. In contrast, only 9.3 percent of whites did not graduate from high school. Based on the 2000–2050 census projections shown earlier, Murdock concluded that more than half of the US labor force in the future will be today's minorities, suggesting that the economic future of the nation will be strongly tied to how well blacks and Hispanics are educationally prepared today.[29]

There is, arguably, a multiplicity of factors contributing to the poor performance of students, especially in the inner cities, where minority communities predominate. Lack of good parenting is cited in many instances. It is obvious that without strong family support or supervision, children are less likely to acquire the type of discipline that can direct them toward good academic performance. It might also be the case that parents may be too tied up at work to give sufficient attention to their kids at home. Mention should also be made that in some cases, parents may be well intentioned; however,

---

28 "Population Projections of the United States by Age, Sex, Race, and Hispanic Origin: 1995 to 2050," *Current Population Reports*, US Department of Commerce (Refer Table M. Population by Age, Race, and Hispanic Origin: 1990 to 2050), accessed May 16, 2014, www.census.gov/prod/1/pop/p25-1130/p251130.pdf.

29 These data were part of the presentation by Steve H. Murdock at the 2011 Conference on The Future of State Universities, accessed June 18, 2012, www.futureofstateuniversities.com/video. Murdock is a demographer and the director of the US Bureau of the Census, 2007–2009.

they may not be sufficiently educated themselves to assist their children with schoolwork. A persistent problem in some families in the inner cities is the absence of one or both parents owing to incarceration and substance abuse. This vacuum makes it difficult for children to grow up wholesomely. Finally, and equally worthy of mention, is the fact that kids may perform poorly at school in spite of their parents' best efforts. Any and all of these factors could adversely impact childhood education in a significant way.

The prevalence of street crimes poses the greatest danger to children, especially those who live in the inner cities. In many low-income neighborhoods that are laden with gangs and where the youth can be killed simply for gym shoes or a leather jacket, kids have nowhere safe to spend time outside of school. In some cases, they are forced to join a gang. Saying no to gang membership is often not an option because those who refuse to join usually incur the wrath of the gang leaders. These social hindrances stand in the way of a successful educational experience for any child.

For many inner city kids, especially those from single-parent homes, these challenges add to the problem of poverty, which has been cited in many studies as a prime contributor to the poor academic performance of grade school students.[30] In 2011, Teach for America published a report showing that only half of low-income students will graduate from high school by age 18. And those who make it through high school will perform, on average, at an eighth-grade level.[31]

A Gold Medal for Teachers

The state of public schools—especially with respect to the quality of instruction and student learning—is undoubtedly the thorniest issue in childhood

---

30 An insightful summary of studies on the role of poverty in children's educational performance is contained in "Single Parent Households and Childhood Academic Achievement" by Katherine Jones, Yahoo!Voices, September 7, 2007, http://voices.yahoo.com/single-parent-households-childhood-academic-achievement-524122.html?cat=4.

31 Teach for America (TFA) is an organization that recruits recent college graduates to teach at failing public schools. Their data, published in 2011, also show that only 10 percent of students growing in poverty will graduate from college. Referenced in USA Today, April 18, 2011, www.usatoday.com/news/opinion/forum/2011-04-18-school-vouchers-worth-a-shot.htm.

academic achievement. Back in the 1990s, I had a firsthand encounter with the deplorable state of some of our public schools when I joined a predominantly African-American church at Chicago's southwest side. My main draw to this church was its heavy emphasis on youth mentoring. Through my involvement in this church's mentoring program, I learned of the sad state of the public schools in which my mentees were enrolled. All of my mentees were from single-parent low-income households. Many of the students at these schools spoke with disturbingly poor grammar. I was also quite appalled by the students' choice of wardrobe, which I thought was better suited for a hip-hop concert or perhaps even a circus show. The apathy of some of the teachers was evident. I must hasten to add, however, that the great majority of the teachers appeared quite capable.

In my view, a learning environment should be a place of high excellence. No parent should have to settle for less, and no child should expect anything less. The training of the human mind is the greatest and most fundamental industry in human existence. I am ever impressed by the motto of the United Negro College Fund (UNCF), which declares that "a mind is a terrible thing to waste." This motto, I believe, recognizes the grave danger of denying anyone the right to quality and competitive education. I believe that this point of view raises the stakes for all educators, who must accept the prime responsibility for molding and mentoring the child.

Consider this: in a manufacturing plant, you can make one or two defective widgets and still remain profitable. All you have to do is throw away the bad widgets, retool the machine, and continue with production. What would you do if you "produced" a failed student? Throw him away like a defective widget? But all too often, this is what happens in many of our public schools. Children who cannot perform for one reason or another are easily tossed out. The result is the frightening population of inner city kids in penitentiaries. Often, we blame the parents or "society" for the reasons mentioned earlier. A few demagogues on national television and on church pulpits prefer to blame the government. In all of this, little is said about those who are directly responsible for *teaching* the pupils.

I sometimes ask myself the following question: If I were a craftsman and through the years a good number of my products kept turning out defective, should my competency for that occupation not be called to question? I worry that this notion of occupational responsibility appears not to hold—at least not as strongly—when it comes to teachers in the classroom. In our corporations and organizations, those in charge are expected, and often required, to take responsibility for the outcome of their operations. We hold CEOs accountable for their firms' performance, even in cases where they may not be directly responsible for a weak outcome. Physicians often lose their license for the least instance of medical malpractice. Church leadership is held liable for the conduct of the clergy. And, for good measure, the president of the United States hardly gets a pass whenever the economy falters, regardless of how the economic weakness came about. Somehow, however, we seem reluctant to hold teachers to the same high level of responsibility for the performance of the students in their care.

I am often troubled by the direction of discussions in the media concerning the state of our public schools. Often, these discussions focus on the welfare of teachers and the demands of teachers unions rather than the quality of education and student performance. As a teacher myself, I favor all arguments that teachers deserve to be well paid, protected, and respected. Teachers, after all, have the awesome responsibility of shaping the minds of our children—who are, pardon the cliché, the *leaders of tomorrow*. But to place the welfare of a teacher ahead of that of a child is, to say the least, tragic. The teacher can lose his or her job and go on to seek another employment. But a child who has lost out on a decent education is lost to society forever.

A well-known and rather sad fact is that teachers are poorly paid. No arguments here. There is no country in the world that I know of where teachers get the pay they so rightly deserve. But, truth be told, what your occupation pays in a free-market economy is ultimately the result of demand and supply. Like any other job, teachers are rewarded based not only on the value of their occupation but also on the available number of qualified individuals ready and willing to do the job. The value of the teaching occupation is very high and, I daresay, higher than that of most other occupations. But the availability of qualified individuals willing to enter the profession is equally very high. This is the Economics 101 of the low teacher pay.

I remember a not-too-pleasant discussion I once had with my dean early in my career as an academic. I complained that I was underpaid compared to my colleagues elsewhere who also hold doctoral degrees in my field. My dean, with a gentle and what may have also been a condescending smile, suggested that if I became a college professor for the pay, I should rethink my career decision. I might not have liked the answer I received, but I knew the response was right on the money (no pun intended).

Teaching is unlike any other profession. There cannot be half measures in ensuring that students succeed. To produce a successful student, one must not only be a good teacher but also a caring mentor. This is especially vital at the primary to middle school levels because children at this stage are still in their formative years and are impressionable. Their future academic success or failure relies heavily on how they are guided in the earlier years.

In a study of what causes students to drop out of high school, a Johns Hopkins University researcher, Robert Balfanz, found that the signs appear much earlier, while the student is in middle school. He found, in particular, that sixth graders with a record of truancy, bad conduct, and poor performance have a three-in-four chance of later dropping out of high school. Balfanz then concluded that to cut down on the high school dropout rate, it is important to intervene early, in middle school.[32] An example of such early intervention is a special student care program instituted by Middle School 224 in the Bronx, New York (featured in PBS *Frontline* on July 18, 2012). The success of this program is evident in that regardless of the emotional and social impediments students may come with, they can still do well if teachers take the primary responsibility to ensure their success. To always blame parents and society, and to look to other factors as an excuse for the poor performance of students, should not be accepted under any circumstance. While these other factors may be tenable, they ought not to be used as a crutch in addressing poor student performance in public schools.

There was a television news program sometime in the 1990s about how some cab drivers in New York City and Washington, DC, were reluctant to pick up African American passengers. One of the cabbies in the interview explained that the reluctance was due to the risk of getting mugged by a black passenger. The follow-up question by the interviewer

---

32 Ruth Curran Neild, Robert Balfanz, and Liza Herzog, "An Early Warning System," *Educational Leadership: Early Intervention at Every Age* 65, no. 2 (October 2007): 28–33.

went something like, "If you think the job is too risky for you, why then did you choose to be a cab driver in the first place?" I suppose the key takeaway from this exchange was that by choosing to be a cabbie, the driver should also accept the responsibilities and challenges that go with that occupation. It would be imprudent to base one's failure at a job on the hazards of the occupation, especially if those hazards are well-known prior to making the choice to enter that occupation.

This notion of professional responsibility is particularly central in the teaching profession. Teaching is perhaps the one profession where the advancement of human civilization rests squarely on the hand of one individual—the teacher. Such an awesome responsibility ought to cause one to rethink the advisability of choosing such a profession. Yet, the millions who have excelled in it can point to no other occupation that leaves one with a greater sense of accomplishment.

In my experience — both as a student and as a teacher — a good teacher is someone who is trusted and looked up to by students. Students rely on the teacher to help, guide, and prepare them for life. The students' future relies squarely on how the teacher molds and nurtures them. I believe that such manner of mentoring can overcome most weaknesses students may come with. It is little wonder that most people, when asked, are quick to name a grade school teacher as the person who was most impactful in their lives growing up. You could not pay anyone enough—in cash or in kind—for the work of a good and caring teacher. Like my dean kindly counseled, if money and the niceties of a noble career are the driving force for anyone, the teaching profession should certainly not be considered as an employment option. I believe it is essential that universities with primary and secondary education programs include in their curriculum a healthy dose of income and career expectations for the teaching profession.

I have great admiration for the thousands of teachers and counselors who continue to make a difference in the lives of students. I am particularly inspired by my own mother, who was also my first grade teacher and who, because of her love for children, was called "Mom" by many of her students as well as some of her younger peers. Initially it bothered me that other kids competed with my siblings and me in this manner. But the depth of respect and appreciation embedded in that reference soon became a point of pride for all of us in my family. My mother hardly made enough money from her teaching employment. She retired without any savings but with a reservoir of satisfaction from the difference she made in the lives of hundreds of children over the years. In her retirement years, her social security is us, her children.

Much can be learned about the great sacrifice good teachers make from watching the documentary movie *Waiting for Superman*. It is true that the movie brings out many things that are disquieting about our public schools and teachers unions. But it also points to some very creative things many fine educators and administrators around the country are doing to help students succeed.

I admire the vision and courage of Michelle Rhee, former chancellor of Washington, DC, Public Schools (2007–2010). She challenged teachers to a higher level of performance and, in 2010, offered them incentive compensation in exchange for tenure. Unfortunately, her proposal was never even brought up for discussion, let alone a vote, by the teachers union. Rhee was compelled to quit her position, but she moved on to found *StudentFirst*, a nonprofit advocacy organization that works on education reform issues. It is equally regrettable that the incumbent Washington, DC mayor at the time, Adrian Fenty, who hired Rhee, lost his reelection bid at the Democratic primaries mayoral election in 2010. It was rather ironic that many parents and community leaders in Washington, DC, mostly in the African American community, blamed Mayor Fenty for hiring a chancellor who was too aggressive. Meanwhile, the graduation rates for African-American students in Washington, DC, public schools remain below the national average for African-American students and significantly less than the national average for all students.[33]

Perhaps one of the most successful teachers of our time is Geoffrey Canada, founder of Harlem's Children Zone. Canada, who grew up in the tough South Bronx neighborhood of New York City, knows firsthand the incapacities that go with poverty and violence in the inner cities. His innovative mentoring and very successful teaching methods have earned him several awards and recognitions. His initiatives have also proved that

---

33 *"The State of the District of Columbia Public Schools 2010: A Five Year Update,"* A report of the Washington Lawyers' Committee for Civil Rights and Urban Affairs, August 2010, accessed May 18, 2014, www.washlaw.org/pdf/DC%20Public%20Schools-5%20Year%20Update%20-%20Final.pdf.

students can succeed regardless of their socioeconomic barriers. There is no stronger advocate for children than this man.

Oprah Winfrey, who needs no introduction beyond her name, has worked tirelessly through the years to support quality education around the country and beyond. She puts her money where her mouth is, giving away millions of dollars to countless educational endeavors. In the final season of the *Oprah Winfrey Show* in 2010, she gave the last $6 million from her Angel Network to six of the best performing charter schools in the country. A good number of her shows were dedicated to celebrating award winning teachers around the country. I was particularly impressed by the honor she paid them in her final season, on September 21 and 24, 2010.

A New Direction

Going forward, I believe we must confront two key imperatives if childhood education is to be salvaged for the benefit of the country's future. The first is that teachers should really take a backseat and consider student success and achievement as a nonnegotiable priority. Many teachers unions are so dug-in in their demands that often, it is the welfare of the teachers rather than that of the students that is preeminent in their negotiations with local authorities. I daresay that the cost of lost learning to students in the days that teachers have gone on strike far exceeds whatever the benefits the unions might have gained from their industrial actions. Nevertheless, this view in no way suggests that teachers should just sit back and accept any conditions of employment stipulated by local authorities. Instead, it argues against the frequent use of work stoppages as the weapon of choice in their collective bargaining.

The second and perhaps more important imperative is that we must accept, although sadly, the permanence of the socioeconomic challenges that kids, especially those from the inner cities, come with. We can blame parents and society all we want, but the dynamics have remained unchanged through the years. In accepting this reality, we should steer the conversation on public education to innovative yet simple ways that can be employed to effectively educate the child.

One of my favorite stories in this aspect is of a kid from the South Side of Chicago named Odion. I had the privilege of mentoring this individual in the 1990s and 2000s. Odion attended one of the badly run-down public schools in Chicago's South Side and, like many kids his age, had very little incentive to complete grammar school let alone continue on to college. If he went to college, he would be the first to do so in his extended family. Fortunately, his connection to disciplined mentoring kept him in check. Odion worked every summer, which kept him away from street gangs. Having a job also taught him how to be financially responsible early on. The intervention of the church, which kept him occupied on most weekends, instilled self-discipline in him. Because of the support and guidance he received, Odion went on to graduate from the University of Illinois in 2011 with a degree in community health. Two years later, he earned a master's degree in health administration at Indiana University Bloomington.

Odion's story is not at all unique. His continued progress, which serves society well, can easily be replicated by providing the same conditions that made his personal and academic success possible. The conditions that ensure success are almost always the same ones that imbue discipline and responsibility in everyone. These are values that are taught at home, by parents. However, the reality is that there are many kids who do not have that family support structure. Caught between a myriad of problems on the streets and an uncertain learning environment at school, a working solution could explore the benefits of military-style academies. In addition to offering students with year-round boarding, such institutions of learning would also require smart common attire. Uniforms would have to be made by designated tailors and sewn in a way that encourages students to dress properly with polished shoes, blazers, slacks, button-down shirts, and ties. These are simple aspects of appearance that elevate one's image in society and build self-esteem.

I find that how one dresses often influences a person's self-image and therefore how a person acts in the public arena. Even in distant and not-so-rich countries like Thailand, Ghana, and Haiti, I have observed that when students are smartly dressed in their fine school uniforms, they exude an unmistakable sense of pride. Such appearances eliminate grounds for antagonism by other students since everybody is dressed the same way. It is sometimes the case that in some of our public schools students are distracted by the more expensive and perhaps more fashionable attire worn by others. These distractions take away from the type of disciplined and focused learning environment that should be in place in an educational institution.

Boarding regulations that are designed in the fashion of a military academy require a higher threshold of competency for teachers. I think teacher training would have to include specific ways to mentor and manage students in residence. As I see it, such a guarded learning environment offers students six key benefits. First, it would provide a disciplined environment that helps foster a healthy development of the mind. In this sense, I am reminded of the UNCF motto that "a mind is a terrible thing to waste." Second, students are taught and assigned chores that help them acquire or for some, reinforce independent living skills. They learn, in particular, how to take care of themselves, as well as how to be of service to others. Third, students are given lessons in social etiquette and simple courtesies, which are essential in professional and social relationships. Fourth, students are taught grooming skills such as appearing clean shaven with shined shoes and dressing for success, and what I call the four *p*'s of good manners: polished, professional, punctual, and polite. Fifth, students go through physical drills that promote health and fitness. And, finally, by living in year-round boarding schools, students from high-crime neighborhoods are able to escape gang life and unhealthy relationships, which often result in high mortality rates, felony convictions, and—just as serious—unwanted pregnancies.

I am not a fan of coeducational boarding schools at the grammar school level. Proponents of coeducational schools argue that they are a microcosm of society. They point to the fact that since men and women interact in both at home and in the workplace, coed schools can be an environment in which gender differences are better understood. This is a compelling, but regretfully, impractical point of view. I prefer to consider this matter at ground level. Anybody who has been to any of the inner city high schools would agree that they are anything but the ideal environments for learning these fine attributes. I am not a sociologist, and I do not claim to begin to understand the full dynamics of interpersonal relationships. However, I have mentored quite a few inner city adolescents long enough to know that young men are easily distracted by girls and often succumb to social complexes that keep them from concentrating in the classroom. In a class by themselves, young men are relieved of these distractions.

A healthy educational environment is one that is disciplined and controlled. While a year-round boarding school would undoubtedly cost taxpayers quite a bit, the ultimate payoff is worth its weight in gold. In any event, we have not had much cause to celebrate under the current dispensation, where many public school systems, like Washington, DC's, spent more than $18,000 per student in 2010 alone.[34] On the other hand, we should not be more satisfied with spending millions of dollars to incarcerate young felons and then act like Charles Dickens's Ebenezer Scrooge when it comes to providing top-notch education for America's children. Ultimately, it is a matter of dollars and sense. If we invest money the right way—to educate and build up the child—our society, by and large, will be the better for it.

---

34 "Public Education Finances: 2010," US Census Bureau, accessed September 20, 2012, www2.census.gov/govs/school/10f33pub.pdf. The exact amount spent by DC public schools, per student, was $18,667, which was the highest of any school district. For the country at large, the cost was $10,615 per pupil.

PART II

PERSONAL FINANCIAL PRUDENCE

Chapter 5. Financial Planning

Live within your means. Never be in debt. And by husbanding your money, you can always lay it out well. But when you get in debt you become a slave. Therefore I say to you never involve yourself in debt, and become no man's surety.

—Andrew Jackson

When our income is hardly enough to pay for personal living expenses and outstanding debt, we need a financial plan. To me, a financial plan is not just a tool designed to ensure we live within our means but also a roadmap to a debt-free life. While education planning is key to ensuring a good quality of life in the future, how effectively we manage the incomes we earn from our employments ultimately determines whether that quality of life is attainable. In an earlier chapter, I presented a financial planning model for determining how much to save for education. In this chapter, I present a general framework for planning for other important personal financial goals, the most important of which is retirement. Retirement planning is discussed exclusively in the next chapter.

Planning to Buy a Home

A good financial plan outlines the expected cash inflows and outflows over a future period. Businesses use it as a model for determining the viability of an intended investment. For individuals, it serves as a wise means to ensure that any financial decision made today lines up with a specific financial goal. For example, a financial plan may be used for education, a wedding, purchase of property, and retirement, just to name a few. More importantly, it also allows one to determine whether a planned expenditure is within one's financial capacity.

I remember a conversation I had with a former student of mine in the summer of 2001. She and her husband wanted to know how much to set aside, periodically, toward the purchase of their first home. They planned to make the purchase within three years. To better understand the size and value of their intended home, as well as other financial obligations they had, I began by asking some basic questions, which went something like this:

Question: Where do you intend to buy the property?

Answer: Somewhere in Northwest Indiana, preferably in the Town of Munster.

Question: Are you looking at a home of a certain square footage, and if so, how much?

Answer: Yes, between 1,500 and 2,500 square feet.

Question: Based on the size of home and the location, you're probably looking at a purchase price of no less than about $250,000, right?

Answer: That sounds about right.

Question: Do you have any money already saved up toward the down payment?

Answer: No, that's what we would like to figure out, as well as monthly mortgage payments.

My advice: To avoid paying personal mortgage insurance on the home loan, you would need a down payment of at least 20 percent of the home price. So, for a home costing $250,000, you need no less than $50,000 as down payment. Since you are looking to make the purchase in three years, you need to put away about $1,400 per month for the next thirty-six months to reach that goal.

At this information, they both flinched. However, they were also smart to ask whether I took into account interest compounding on their planned monthly savings. Unfortunately, at the time, the most you could earn on any short-term interest-bearing bank account was no more than about 2 percent per year (interest rates on savings accounts continued to fall to near zero in the few years following the 2008 financial crisis). I explained to them that when interest rates were as low as they were, it was wise to overestimate how much to put away, periodically, toward a financial goal.

More importantly, considering that a closing cost of up to $4,000 might be required on the settlement date, the monthly investments would probably need to be kicked up a bit more to ensure that the saved amount was sufficient to pay for both the down payment as well as the closing cost. By the time they left my office on that lovely summer day, they realized they either needed to downsize their dream home or wait a little while longer before making a purchase.

By the way, this couple could also have opted to shoot for a lower down payment. However, doing so would raise their monthly mortgage payments, which also would include a personal mortgage insurance premium. Further, if they went for a lower down payment, they would run the risk of falling behind on their mortgage payment if, for any reason, their income declined. Many homeowners with little upfront equity on their properties found themselves in this predicament in 2007 as home prices and personal incomes fell across the country. It is important to remember that a total house payment includes not only mortgage (interest and part principal) but also personal mortgage insurance (if the down payment is less than 20 percent of the home price), homeowner's insurance, and property taxes.

Being able to afford the total house payment is only one piece of the financial story. One should also be able to afford living in it. There are a host of other living expenses a homeowner must contend with, all of which must be articulated in a financial plan.

Designing a Financial Plan

A financial plan is a template that lines up take-home income against all expenses. It is a reality check for two key reasons. First, it recognizes all the legitimate cash flows—receipts and payments—for each month. Second, it tells whether someone is living within his or her means. In many cases, a financial plan is prepared using monthly data, in keeping with the fact that most bills are paid monthly.

Part 1 of the Financial Plan

It is helpful to view a financial plan as a three-part document. The first part displays three pieces of information: take-home income, what you own, and what you owe. What you own are your liquid assets, which are essentially savings and checking account balances that are readily available to pay for day-to-day living expenses. Liquid assets do not include long-term investments such as those designed for retirement, education, and other financial goals with a long-term horizon. Also, fixed assets such as homes, furniture, and cars are excluded since, realistically, those would not be liquidated just to pay for daily living expenses.

Likewise, what you owe should include only liquid liabilities, consisting of credit card charges (as well as other personal debt), overdue medical bills, and past due education loans. They do not include home loans and car notes if those are still current. It is not necessary to list home and automobile loan balances here since their payoff follows a regular and prearranged schedule. Loan payments for home and automobile are part of the monthly recurring expenses, which, along with other expenses, would be considered in the final part (part three) of the financial plan.

The following example considers an individual with an annual income of $43,000 and an average tax rate of 30 percent. If you subtract 30 cents for every dollar earned and then divide the result by twelve, you will find that the after-tax take-home monthly income is approximately $2,500. This amount is the first piece of information that appears on the first section of the financial plan. Note that take-home income, not gross income, is considered on a financial plan. Take-home is your disposable income, the amount from which all living expenses are paid.

Table 5.1. Financial Plan Part 1: Income and Liquid Balance Sheet

Monthly Take-Home	$2,500
What I Own	
Checking	$1,500
Savings	$1,500
Total	$3,000
What I Owe	
Credit card 1	$1,000
Credit card 2	$6,000
Past due debt	$10,000
Education loan (past due)	$20,000
Total	$37,000
Net Surplus/Deficit	-$34,000

This example shows that this individual has total liquid assets of $3,000. The total debt that must be paid off in short order is $37,000. Assuming that the savings of $3,000 is directed to debt payoff, there is still a net deficit of $34,000. This is a bad report for this individual. As such, the budget section of the financial plan should additionally address the payoff of this deficit plus any interest charges that may accrue as a result.

Part 2 of the Financial Plan

The disposable (take-home) income of $2,500 is carried forward to part two of the financial plan. From this amount, the contributions to each of the personal investments are made. These include retirement, dependents' education, emergency savings, and other needed investments. This part of the financial plan is what some refer to as "pay yourself first" because the contributions are for future personal financial goals. The following is a demonstration of how to outline the key investments that should appear on a financial plan.

Table 5.2. Financial Plan Part 2: Personal Investments

Item	Suggested % of Income	Amount
Take-home income (from Part 1)		$2,500
Investments:		
Long-term investment	10%	$250
College savings	5%	$125
Emergency and short-term savings	5%	$125
Retirement savings	5%	$125
Residual		$1,875

In this example, we find that this individual dedicates 10 percent of take-home pay toward long-term investments. In general, these are investments lasting ten years or longer, and are typically held in a well-diversified stock mutual fund. Mutual funds such as this mimic the performance of the broad US stock market and go by names such as stock index, equity index, and S&P 500. For a variety of reasons, it is advisable that about a tenth of take-home pay go into long-term savings. In this example, the remaining investments are set to five percent of take-home income. Education contribution is typically for a minor and is made as part of a college savings plan, discussed in an earlier chapter.[35]

In addition to other short-term savings goals, the emergency savings is where to withdraw funds for household payments in the event of a temporary income loss. It also serves as a source of funds for contingencies. In my view, it is prudent to ensure that emergency savings equal about one year of total household expenditures. Some financial advisers recommend a period of six to nine months. However, the employment challenges that persisted for years after the 2008 financial crisis suggest that it is wise to overestimate contributions to this account.

Emergency savings may be held in the same account as other short-term investments. Short-term investments, in general, are those used to satisfy financial goals of no longer than a year or two. Because funds held as short-term investments could be pulled out in short order, it is advisable to place them in low-risk interest-bearing assets. Examples are money market deposit accounts (offered by banks and savings institutions), money market mutual funds (offered by investment companies), and certificates of deposits (offered by banks, credit unions, and savings institutions).

Retirement contribution is what goes into the individual retirement account (IRA) or similar investment. A personal retirement investment, like an IRA, is set up only as a supplement to employee pension and employer-sponsored retirement plans. The typical employer-sponsored plans are 401(k), 401(a), or 403(b). The process for determining how much to set aside each month for retirement investment is discussed in the next chapter.

Part 3 of the Financial Plan

The third and final part of the financial plan itemizes all recurring monthly expenses in a budget format. The list begins with the must-pay expenses. These are the scheduled payoff of any outstanding credit card balances and

---

35 Most finance experts would agree that the best vehicle today for college savings is a 529 Education Plan. A good place to begin is www.savingforcollege.com. Please note that the data presented here are for illustration only.

past due debt, followed by regular payments on current loans such as mortgage and car note. The remaining items in this section are the routine monthly expenses, such as food, telephone, transportation, utilities, and personal care.

Continuing from the preceding example, after the monthly investment contributions have been accounted for, this individual is left with $1,875. From this residual, payments are made toward debt payoff as well as other recurring monthly expenses. Accordingly, the first items in this budget section are the mandatory debt repayments, beginning with a scheduled payoff of the liability items listed in Part 1 of the financial plan. The minimum amount to pay for each of the outstanding liabilities depends on a debt elimination plan that must be worked out separately. The following is only an example of how to incorporate debt payoff into a monthly budget.

Table 5.3. Financial Plan Part 3: Monthly Expenses

Budget Item	Outflow	Balance
Residual balance (from Part 2)		$1,875
Credit card 1	$200	$1,675
Credit card 2	$300	$1,375
Past due debt	$200	$1,175
School loan	$200	$975
Auto loan	$200	$775
Rent	$400	$375
Utilities	$50	$325
Telephone	$60	$265
Food	$150	$115
Gasoline	$100	$15
Auto insurance	$100	-$85
Auto maintenance	$50	-$135
Miscellaneous	$50	-$185

The outcome of this financial plan shows that this individual's financial situation does not look good, to say the least. The final cash balance is negative! Some remedies may include reducing, and perhaps even eliminating, some of the investment contributions in Part 2 of the financial plan. As tight as the budget is already, this individual may also consider cutting back on discretionary items such as food, telephone, and miscellaneous spending. Seeking additional income from a second job is always a wise idea in a case like this. These are tough choices, made even tougher by the fact that more than half of the recurring outflows goes toward debt payoff. Notwithstanding, the financial plan has done its job—by revealing the challenges and options this individual faces going forward.

The numeric example shown above brings into view a financial problem that is common to many, if not most, of us; and that is the creation of consumer debt through the use of credit cards. The real problem though is that when credit cards—instead of cash—are used to pay for personal spending, there is the danger that income limitations might be ignored. This problem might not arise if cash is used. Perhaps it is in this respect that the old saying is true: cash is king. Notwithstanding, there are circumstances when the use of credit cards is beneficial. Those will be addressed in the chapter on how to manage personal debt.

Chapter 6: Planning for Life and Death

Retirement is like a long vacation in Las Vegas. The goal is to enjoy it to the fullest, but not so fully that you run out of money.

—Jonathan Clements

Today in America, we are living longer than ever before. With a longer life expectancy, how does one know that enough money is being saved up for retirement? And if you are the breadwinner in your family, how do you know your dependents will be well cared for if something were to happen to you?

Two key aspects of financial planning discussed in this chapter are retirement and life insurance. Retirement planning is an investment program designed to ensure there is sufficient money during one's retirement years. Life insurance, on the other hand, is a financial program designed to take care of the financial needs of one's dependents upon his or her death.

It is important to emphasize that a life insurance policy should never be mistaken for an investment. While life insurance provides for one's dependents in the event of untimely death, an investment program, like retirement savings, provides income during one's lifetime. So it is easily seen that these two financial products differ in a life and death way, so to speak.

Many life insurance products feature what I call pseudo-investments. Examples are annuities and cash value life insurance. However, it is not a good idea to use life insurance as a vehicle to meet retirement or any other investment needs. Investments should be held exclusively so as to minimize the cost of maintaining them. Also, by targeting an investment to its specific goal, it makes it easier to determine how much is required to attain that goal. This process is detailed in the following section dealing with retirement planning.

Planning for Retirement

Retirement investment is widely considered the most important type of investment because it is where a post-worklife financial future is secured. For this reason, retirement planning is critical if financial hardship is to be avoided during one's retirement years. Conventional retirement savings programs include an employee pension, 401(a), 403(b), 401(k), 457 plan, individual retirement account (IRA), Simplified Employee Pension (SEP), and Keogh plan. The last two are for the self-employed and unincorporated businesses.

If available, an employer-sponsored 401(k) is the most beneficial retirement plan because often, the employer matches the employee's contribution up to a predefined maximum. For example, suppose an employer promises to contribute 50 cents for every dollar an employee pays into a 401(k), up to a maximum of $1,000 per month. This means that if the employee invests $800 of his or her own money in any given month, the employer will contribute 50 percent of that amount into the account, which is $400—for a total of $1,200. To take full advantage of the employer's matching, therefore, it is smart to contribute at least $2,000 because half of it is $1,000, the maximum amount the employer will add, under the arrangement. With such a plan, the employee instantly earns a 50 percent rate of return on the retirement investment without lifting a finger. And, of course, the tax deferral feature of these retirement plans is an additional bonus.

Pension plans, if available, are offered by the employer. Also, employer-sponsored retirement plans such as a 401(k) and 403(b) are set up by the employer. For the most part, an IRA is the only retirement plan that is initiated and funded solely by the individual. For this reason, it goes by the name *individual* retirement account. It is wise to view an IRA only as supplementary retirement savings and not as the primary vehicle for retirement savings. This is because while both IRAs and employer-sponsored programs are tax deferred, the employer-sponsored programs have greater savings benefits because of the matching feature. Notwithstanding, the employer is not bound to match the employee's 401(k) contributions to any extent. The matching feature is simply designed as a form of incentive compensation. It could also be viewed as a way to encourage the employee to save toward retirement.

An important fact about IRAs is that there are two types to choose from: Traditional and Roth. Traditional IRA contributions are tax-deductible in the year they are made. That is, these contributions can be deducted from gross income, which helps reduce how much tax to pay for that year. Taxes are paid on the traditional IRA only when withdrawals are made during retirement. Higher tax rates in the future will therefore have a negative impact on the growth of this type of tax-deferred investment.

Contributions on the Roth are after-tax. As a result, these contributions may be withdrawn at any time without taxes or penalties. Making a withdrawal before the minimum retirement age or before the required minimum length of time to hold the investment (called vesting period) may result in taxes and penalties, but only on the income portion of the withdrawal. Otherwise, Roth IRA withdrawals—both the original contributions and the accumulated earnings—are tax free at retirement.

With a Roth IRA, the money may be left in the account for any length of time so that it grows larger as a person ages. By contrast, withdrawals from a traditional IRA are required once a person turns 70.5 years of age. This is another reason some view the Roth IRA as a better retirement vehicle than the Traditional IRA. But there are income limitations with the Roth. The higher the income, the less likely one is to qualify for the Roth. Tax laws change constantly, though. Therefore, it is important to speak with a tax or financial advisor for the most current updates on these two retirement plans.[36]

It is helpful to view an IRA as a plan designed to fill the gap between the accumulated amount of work-based retirement plans and one's retirement savings target. Without this manner of reckoning, there is a possibility that one could undersave for retirement. This concept is the basis of the retirement savings example I show later in this chapter.

One thing, however, that all retirement plans have in common is that contributions must come from an earned income. That is, one has to have a paid employment—from which to retire in the future—to be allowed to

---

36 Tax regulations regarding retirement plans change from time to time. No views expressed here should be considered a golden rule. It is best to confer with a financial advisor before making any form of investment.

have a retirement account. The goal is to ensure that a retired worker has enough money saved up during his or her retirement years.

As it turns out, more and more Americans fall into the trap of under-saving for retirement. Because of this, many workers have no choice but to prolong their working years. On March 9, 2010, *CNNMoney* reported that 43 percent of American workers in 2010 had less than $10,000 saved up for retirement. A majority of those surveyed said their minimum retirement savings goal was $250,000, meaning there is yet a big savings gap to cover for a good number of us.[37] To address this problem, I offer the following retirement savings model designed to answer the key question: Will I have enough money saved up when I retire?

Saving for Retirement

Saving for retirement takes into account four important factors, which are also the steps for retirement planning. The first is to determine how many years a person expects to live once in retirement. This, of course, has to be in sync with one's life expectancy.[38] The second is to figure out how much money to withdraw from the retirement portfolio during each year of retirement. It is important to project an income level that will ensure the same standard of living as would be maintained during one's best worklife.[39] The third is to calculate the desired retirement savings goal, which is how much the individual would like to have saved up at the point of retirement. Note, this amount has to be sufficient to provide

---

37 CNN Money, *43% have less than $10k for retirement*, accessed February 12, 2012, CNN, http://money.cnn.com/2010/03/09/pf/retirement_confidence. This CNN report was based on the annual Retirement Confidence Survey conducted by the Employee Benefit Research Institute.

38 The US Social Security Administration provides online calculators for life expectancy as well as retirement age (www.socialsecurity.gov/planners/lifeexpectancy.htm).

39 I hold the anecdotal view, as do some financial planners, that to maintain their worklife standard of living in retirement, retirees will need to replace about 80 percent of their pre-retirement after-tax income. For example, suppose the annual after-tax worklife income is $50,000. In retirement, the individual will need about $40,000 per year, to ensure a roughly constant standard of living. This assumes most household debts have been paid off.

the annual retirement incomes that were projected in the second step. The fourth and last step is to calculate how much to save up each year or each month during the working years in order to reach the savings goal. I demonstrate this process with the working example presented below.

Step 1. Life Expectancy

In retirement planning, we should work backward, as outlined in the above steps. Consider a forty-year-old man. He plans to retire at age sixty-seven. Based on his life expectancy, he estimates he can live for another twenty-two years beyond the age of retirement (that is, he expects to live to about age eight-nine). Factors such as family history, personal lifestyle, and health conditions are among many that normally influence life expectancy.

Step 2. Retirement Income

Suppose that during his years of retirement, this individual desires to withdraw $3,500 per month from his retirement portfolio. Multiplied by twelve, this gives him an annual take-home retirement income of $42,000. Note that this income projection does not include Social Security payments, which, upon retirement, will be an additional source of income. The monthly figure of $3,500 in this example is, therefore, the estimate of the amount that would be added to Social Security income upon retirement. It may be helpful to note that the average monthly Social Security benefit for a retired American worker was about $1,230 at the beginning of 2012.[40] Each person's estimated future Social Security payment is shown on a personalized statement sent out periodically by the Social Security Administration.

Step 3. Savings Goal

Assume this individual can earn 3 percent per year, on average, on his investments *during* his retirement years. With the aid of a financial

---

40 Frequently Asked Questions, "*What is the average monthly Social Security benefit for a retired worker?*" Social Security Administration, accessed December 1, 2014, https://faq.ssa.gov/ics/support/KBAnswer.asp?questionID=1802&hitOffset=52+43+31+18+17+16+8+7+6&docID=6836. Note that this amount changes monthly based on the total amount of all benefits paid and the total number of people receiving benefits.

calculator, we can determine that the value of his portfolio at age 67, when he retires, is approximately $669,350. For those who delight in a bit of financial mathematics, this calculation is the present value of $42,000 received each year for 22 years at 3 percent.

Table 6.1. Retirement Planning Part 1: Portfolio Value at Age of Retirement

Intended retirement age	67
Years of retirement	22
Desired annual retirement income	$42,000
Average annual portfolio percentage return	3%
Calculated portfolio value at retirement	$669,350

Next, our role-player needs to find out how much he currently has in all his retirement investments—that is, his pension, 401(k), SEP, 403(b), IRA, etc. Suppose that altogether he currently has $50,000 saved up. Given that he is currently 40 years of age, that means he still has 27 years of worklife left until he retires. During this period, and assuming he makes no additional contributions into any of his retirement plans, he can expect the $50,000 to grow by more than sixfold—based on a 7 percent rate of return per year. The exact future value of the $50,000 for 27 years at 7 percent is $310,693. Since this individual's calculated retirement savings goal is $669,350, it means he will be short by $358,657 (the difference between $669,350 and $310,693).

Table 6.2. Retirement Planning Part 2: Additional Investment to Reach Goal

Retirement portfolio value at current age (40)	$50,000
Current age	40
Years until retirement	27
Expected portfolio percentage return	7%
Value of this portfolio at age of retirement	$310,693
Portfolio shortfall at age of retirement (67)	$358,657

Step 4. Monthly Contributions

Finally, to cover the expected shortfall (of $358,657), our role-player will need to calculate how much he needs to contribute into his retirement savings, each month, between now and age 67. Given the assumed annual portfolio percentage return of 7 percent, his annual contribution comes out to about $4,815, which, when divided by 12 gives a monthly contribution of $401. This type of financial analysis calculates the fixed payments that should be made over a defined period (27 years in this example) at a defined rate of return (7 percent in this example).

Table 6.3. Retirement Planning Part 3: Calculating Monthly Retirement Contribution

Current age	40
Years until retirement	27
Portfolio shortfall at age of retirement (67)	$358,657
Expected portfolio rate of return	7%
Amount to invest per year	$4,815
Amount to invest per month (divide yearly amount by 12)	$401

The calculated monthly investment is the minimum amount that should go into retirement savings between now and the year of retirement in order to meet the retirement savings goal. If one is unable to make the contributions through an employment retirement plan such as 401(k), then an IRA should be used to make these *supplementary* payments to the extent that tax laws allow.

How About Inflation?

There are three caveats in this example. First, it is assumed that this investor already has $50,000 in his retirement portfolio. Note, if currently his portfolio has less than this amount, he will have to increase his monthly contribution to attain his retirement savings goal. The reverse is true if the current portfolio value is greater than $50,000.

Second, we assumed a 7 percent annual investment return until retirement. The value of the retirement portfolio will be larger if he winds up earning more than 7 percent per annum. He will, of course, be short if he earns less than that rate. In many cases, where the remaining worklife is longer than a dozen years, it is possible to earn more than 7 percent per year, on average. This typically occurs if the monthly contributions go into a well-diversified stock mutual fund. Therefore, it is important to ascertain from a financial planner the types of investments that can earn the percentage return used to work out the numbers.

Finally, and most importantly, this analysis assumes that retirement income is a constant $42,000 per year for the 22 years of retirement. This assumption ignores the effect of inflation and could potentially lead to a reduction in one's standard of living as the years go by. For example, suppose this individual withdraws $42,000 at age 68 as well as at age 78. It is obvious that his $42,000 at age 78 will buy fewer goods and services than it did at age 68 if, as is often the case, price levels increase over the years. In view of this, a more realistic retirement income projection should take into account the expected rate of inflation during retirement.

To adjust for inflation, suppose we expect the average inflation rate to be 2 percent per year. Then, given the first year's retirement income of $42,000, the second year's income will have to be $42,840, calculated as $42,000 x (1 + 2%). Likewise, the third will be $43,697, which is calculated as $42,840 x (1 + 2%). Subsequent calculations follow the same pattern. In this way, each year's income reflects a 2 percent inflation rate adjustment. If we carry out these adjustments for the entire 22 years of retirement, the retirement savings goal for this individual, at age 67, will be greater than in the case where the annual withdrawal was the same amount each year. But this also means that he will have to increase his monthly retirement contributions to reach this higher and more realistic savings goal.

Choosing a Retirement Portfolio

Using individual stocks as part of a long-term financial plan—such as retirement and education—is generally not a smart idea. Because an individual firm can go belly-up at any time or just simply perform badly, even over a long period of time, it is safer and better to go with a diversified portfolio of stocks.[41] Such portfolios provide diversification across the types of risks that individually, could bring down a company.

As mentioned earlier, one important way to pursue such prudential investment is to choose a well-diversified stock mutual fund such as one that is based on the Russell 3000 or S&P 500 index. These are broad-based stock indices that capture the general performance of the stocks of the most influential firms in the United States (a significant portion of the incomes of these US firms comes from their international operations). Close to the time of retirement, money can then be gradually shifted into safer investments. Examples of such low risk investments are certificates of deposits, money market mutual funds, and money market deposit accounts. Understandably, these low-risk investments often come with very low interest rates; but that is the price paid for the safety that such investments provide.

About Life Insurance and Property Inheritance

Unlike health insurance, which pays for medical expenses, life insurance pays a death benefit, often a lump sum, to the beneficiaries of the insured person. In my view, the decision to buy life insurance should be based on the existence of three important conditions. One, the insured individual currently has an earned income. Two, the insured individual has dependents such as a spouse, children, or parents who depend on that earned income. And three, the dependents will suffer financial hardship if the insured person passes away. If these three conditions are not satisfied, the insured person has no insurable interest. Without an insurable interest, it is difficult to justify taking out a life insurance policy—unless, of course, the insured person is considered more valuable to the beneficiaries dead than alive.

Life insurance is designed to fill the gap between how much wealth a person has already accumulated and how much financial liability the dependents will incur if that person suddenly passes away. A good investment program should cause one's wealth to increase over time and, as a result, make the need for life insurance to decrease with the passage of time. As a result, it is more important to concentrate on building wealth rather than buying life insurance. Fortunately, these two are not

---

41 Few would disagree that those who invested in auto and airline stocks even as far back as the 1970s have little to rejoice thirty years on.

mutually exclusive in that you can have a life insurance as well as an investment. When one's investments have yet to build up sufficient wealth, a life insurance policy should be in place.

In cases where life insurance is deemed appropriate, only a renewal term life policy makes sense, because only this type of policy is designed as pure life insurance. There are no bells and whistles attached to it. It is important to ensure that a *renewable* clause is built into a term life policy so that regardless of how one's health may have changed over the years, the renewal of the policy is assured.

The face value of a life policy should be approximately equal to how much is required to take care of one's beneficiaries until they become financially independent. It is helpful to consider the following needs when determining the appropriate death benefit for one's policy: home-related expenses, child care, education, and upkeep for the home.

Finally, and to reiterate, buying life insurance as a replacement for a good investment program is unwise. Keep in mind that life insurance is a business, and as a business, insurance companies must earn a profit to remain viable. To earn a profit, they must charge a premium that not only covers the death benefit they must pay if the insured person dies within the policy period, but also the company's operating costs. So, knowing that an insurance premium is an overpayment toward the death benefit should be good reason for one to concentrate on building a personal investment.

Ironically, for many of us, paying a life insurance premium is an easier task than contributing money, periodically, into an investment portfolio. I suppose the reason is because the insurance company will be quick to remind defaulting policyholders of the risk of having their policy annulled. But consider this: if we feed our investment portfolio in as disciplined a manner as we pay the monthly insurance premium, we have a far greater chance of accumulating a decent chunk of money in the future, assuming, of course, that we have invested prudently. All that said, if one is predisposed to a health condition or is engaged in an occupation or hobby that is considered high risk, purchasing life insurance earlier rather than later is a prudent way to protect loved ones.

A comprehensive financial road map should also address other important financial matters such as estate planning, gifts, and property inheritance. Estate planning and property inheritance can be met by setting up a will or, better yet, a living trust since living trusts are simpler and cheaper to implement. Unlike a will, a living trust bypasses the costly and time-consuming process of probate. However, similar to a will, it spells out exactly what a person's desires are in regard to the distribution of his or her assets after death. Note that if one passes away without a will or living trust, that person's property goes to probate, and the courts—not the individual, as would be obvious—will make the decision as to who gets what.

Planning for the future is one sure way to avoid financial hardship both for yourself and your loved ones. Ultimately, the main intent behind financial planning is to avoid the type of financial difficulty that might force a person to become a welfare recipient or, worse still, chronically indebted to some financial institution.

Chapter 7. Managing Personal Debt

Debt is the fatal disease of republics, the first thing and the mightiest to undermine governments and corrupt the people.

—*Wendell Phillips*

In this chapter, I offer some general perspectives on how to make prudent choices concerning personal debt. My mantra going into this discussion is that *money does not create wealth, only brains do.* Being careful not to borrow in excess is a wise way to avoid the pitfalls that dragged us into the 2008 financial crisis.

When we consistently owe more than we earn, we open a Pandora's box that can unleash all kinds of bad things. That was the situation in the years leading up to the collapse of the housing market in 2007. Prior to the housing collapse, total household debt doubled from $7 trillion in 2000 to $14 trillion in 2007. Correspondingly, personal disposable income grew from $7.2 trillion to only $10 trillion, producing a shortfall of $4 trillion just before the crisis erupted.[42] This was the first time in recent history that our collective debt exceeded our earnings by such a wide margin. Given the high level of indebtedness in many households at the

---

42 Data source for household debt: Federal Reserve, "Credit Market Debt Outstanding by Sector," Financial Accounts of the United States, March 6, 2014, accessed May 19, 2014, www.federalreserve.gov/releases/z1/current/accessible/d3.htm.
Data source for personal disposable income: Federal Reserve Bank of St. Louis, "Disposable Personal Income," Economic Research, updated May 1, 2014, accessed May 19, 2014, http://research.stlouisfed.org/fred2/series/DSPI.

time, the stage was set for the massive delinquencies and bankruptcies that would eventually drag down the US economy in 2008.

In a number of my articles published in professional journals, I argued that this unevenness between income and household debt was the chief cause of the financial crisis. As a first concept, debt is created when, for whatever the reason might be, we spend more than we earn. If an individual earns $100 but spends $120, that person is in the hole for twenty bucks. Thus, the only way $120 could actually have been spent is if $20 were borrowed. This new loan adds to whatever existing debt is already in place. If, going forward, enough money can be made to service the debt and eventually pay off the loan, there would be no financial problem, and the use of debt would have been justified in such a case. However, if income fails to keep pace with debt, a disconnect that will eventually lead to a financial crisis will have been created.

The basic lesson on debt, in my view, is to avoid it as much as possible. In Benjamin Franklin's *The Way to Wealth*, he noted that "debt is slavery [and] buying on credit is the road to ruin." This view of debt is as true today as it has ever been. For individuals, it is difficult to see the wisdom in borrowing unless the loan is (1) used to buy items that increase in value over time or (2) invested in assets that are expected to produce income exceeding the cost of the debt. The types of loans that belong in this broad category of so-called good debts include home loans, home improvement loans, business loans, college loans, and in a very restrictive sense, automobile loans.

I will first examine the merits of each of these types of good debts. Next, I will discuss the types of debt that are considered bad. Finally, I will offer a broad guideline on debt elimination.

Good Debt—Home Loans

There are two reasons to justify a home loan. The first is that properties typically rise in value over time (with emphasis on *typically*). For this reason, home improvement loans may also be viewed as an investment since improvements can increase property value and therefore a homeowner's personal equity. The second reason is that for the great majority of us, it is virtually impossible to save up enough money to buy a home. Based on these two premises, a home loan may be justified. The cautionary tale here, though, is to never forget how properties overshot their value prior to the bursting of the price bubble in 2007. From January 2000 to March 2007, the median home price increased by an astounding 60 percent to a record $263,000. It later fell to less than $200,000 in late 2010, following the collapse of the US housing market.[43]

There are four lessons I find insightful with respect to home loans. The first is that home prices do not always go up. A property may already be overpriced at the time of purchase, leaving the homeowner to deal with a subsequent price decline. The second lesson is that it is wise for the home buyer to have a healthy amount of equity in the first place. In the event of foreclosure, a homeowner's equity helps cover any shortfall between the sale price of the property and the loan balance—if prices have declined after the purchase.

For buyers who cannot afford the conventional equity threshold of 20 percent (of the home price), the smart alternative is to seek a less expensive property. The magic number of 20 percent is the real skin in the game for anyone wishing to own a property because if the home is worth less at the time of sale or foreclosure than at the time of purchase, the lender is more likely to recover the amount owed and is therefore less likely to suffer a loss.

When lenders lose money because they recover less than the loan balance, we are all the worse for it. When less money flows in the banking system, a credit crunch is inevitable, as we saw happen in 2008 and 2009. This throws the entire economy into a financial turmoil in which no one benefits. Overall, making an equity down payment of at least 20 percent fetches the best mortgage deals, eliminates personal mortgage insurance, and helps reduce bank distress in the event of foreclosure.

The third lesson about home loans is that total *house payment*—mortgage, property taxes, and homeowner's insurance—should not exceed 30 percent of take-home income. This means that if the homeowner brings home, say, $3,000 per month, the total *house payment* should not exceed $900. In this scenario, the homeowner should still have $2,100 to pay for other living and, if applicable, educational expenses.

In my financial workshops, I counsel that to be on the safe side of

---

43 United States Census Bureau, "Median and Average Sales Prices of New Homes Sold in United States," accessed December 15, 2011, www.census.gov/const/uspriceann.pdf.

debt, one should not buy a home unless total monthly *home-related expenses* are no more than half of take-home pay. Home-related expenses are expenses directly linked to living in the property and include mortgage payment, property taxes, homeowners insurance, personal mortgage insurance (which applies only when down payment is less than 20 percent of home price), electricity, gas, and utilities. Notice that home-related expenses include house payment, as described above, in addition to the listed energy and utilities expenses.

The fourth and final lesson about home loans is that one should maintain sufficient emergency savings. Given the gravity of the financial distress that followed the 2008 financial crisis, I think it is wise to ensure that emergency savings is sufficient to pay for at least twelve months of home-related expenses and perhaps other living expenses such as food, transportation, and telephone. This way, if one is out of a job, he or she would not be hard-pressed to continue to make mortgage and other required household payments. Our collective experience during the Great Recession of 2008–2011 informs us that it took the average American more than a year to find another job that paid at least as much as his or her previous job.

With these caveats in mind, it may be unwise to view home ownership as the fulfillment of the "American dream." This view of home ownership, which led many to acquire home loans beyond their means, is undeniably misleading. Owning a home can be a nightmare if the property is purchased with a loan that is beyond the homeowner's financial capacity. What would be the wisdom in exposing oneself to the possibility of foreclosure if the home loan were to become delinquent?

It is quite possible that for some, if not many, of us, renting is the better option when it comes to finding a place to call home. In any event, the key lesson here is to make a financial choice that can bring peace of mind.

Good Debt—Business Loan

The second good reason to take out a loan is when the funds are invested in an asset that produces a stream of income. For this type of debt to be considered good, the stream of income must exceed the cost of the loan. Also, the safety of the principal must be assured. This type of loan, by definition, is a business loan.

If the borrower owns a business and believes a loan can be used to expand operations and produce a larger income in the future, then perhaps a business loan may be justified. However, just as in any other rational business decision, the borrower must ensure that the expected cash flows from the investment will exceed the interest charges on the loan, as well as pay back the principal. In order for this to happen, the borrower begins by putting together a financial plan for the investment. The plan will detail the projected cash inflows and outflows. The latter includes the interest payments, principal repayment, and the incremental operating costs associated with the investment. There are many websites that provide a guide on how to prepare a financial plan for a business.

Good Debt—Education Loan

As I have shown elsewhere in this book, advanced education lays the foundation for a better job and higher income in the future. For this reason, college education should be considered a vital investment in one's personal and professional development. However, like any good investment, the expected income from postcollege employment must be more than sufficient to pay off the education loan in a timely manner.

Different college majors lead to different careers and income expectations. Therefore, it is important to be mindful of future income when deciding how much money to borrow for college. Notwithstanding, it is prudent to seek grants and scholarships first, before considering education loans. This way, a loan would only be used to pay for what cannot be otherwise covered with free financial assistance. In the earlier chapter on education and income, I laid out the precepts and provided a guide for making an informed education loan decision.

Good Debt—Auto Loan

Using a loan to buy a depreciable asset, like a car, may be good or bad. It is good if it is the only reasonable transportation to work and the job provides enough income to pay off the loan in a timely manner. Otherwise, the loan should, in all likelihood, be considered bad. A car note may be the only option to find the means to get to work right after college, especially where public transportation is unavailable or unreliable. It is also often the case that for most people fresh out of school, there might not be enough personal savings to purchase a car with cash. For these reasons, an auto loan may be the only lifeline to get from point A to point B.

To ensure that the cost of an auto loan is not overbearing, though, it is wise to choose a reliable, previously owned gas-efficient vehicle. Brand new vehicles typically lose about 20 percent of their value the moment the car is driven out of the car dealership. Therefore, buying a good used vehicle may be the wise way to go. To be sure that the auto loan is affordable, the projected monthly car note payment should be included in the financial plan, as outlined in the chapter on financial planning. If the net balance is positive, then all is well.

An auto lease is sometimes a better alternative to an auto loan. By leasing a vehicle, the individual is "borrowing" the car instead of borrowing money to buy it. Leasing may be cheaper than an auto loan if the following conditions apply: (1) the number of miles driven per year is no more than about fifteen thousand; (2) the driver's record is good, and the car can be expected to remain in a fairly good condition with minimal wear and tear through the lease term; (3) intended use time for the vehicle is short, no longer than about four years.

Most auto leases allow for between twelve thousand and fifteen thousand miles per year and are for terms of no longer than four years, perhaps even two or three. The *ownership risk* of a vehicle can be avoided by leasing that vehicle, meaning that one will not be stuck with a tough-to-sell used vehicle when the car is no longer desired. In many cases in which one is unable to make a decent down payment for the purchase of a new vehicle and the above conditions apply, one might find leasing to be the wiser way to go.

Some auto lease programs include a down payment, but that is negotiable. In fact most, if not all, terms in an auto lease are negotiable. Keep in mind, though, that the lower the down payment, the larger the monthly lease payment.

People opposed to auto leasing argue that leasing leaves one with nothing at the end of the lease term, since the car will be returned to the lessor (the leasing company). While this is true, the question really is what difference does it make if the lessee (the individual leasing the car) plans to get a new vehicle at that time? Keep in mind that lease payments are much less than a comparable car loan payment, with the same maturity. The difference in payment, which is the savings on the lease, can accumulate—if carefully planned—to aid in the purchase of another vehicle at the end of the lease term.

There are many individuals who consider it a smart idea to use a home equity loan—instead of a direct auto loan—to finance the purchase of a car. There are two key reasons for this view. The first is that a home equity loan typically carries a lower interest rate than the rate on an auto loan with the same maturity. The second is that interest payments on home loans are tax-deductible, unlike interest payments on auto loans. All that said, *caveat emptor*. This type of loan is a feast or famine. It is true that using a home equity loan to buy a car will save on the interest cost. However, if the borrower defaults for any reason, both the car and the home will be lost!

Bad Debt—Auto Loans and Education Loans

I have already identified conditions in which automobile and education loans are considered good debt. While an auto loan is inevitable in some instances, caution should be applied in making the choice to borrow. I pointed out earlier that because an automobile is a depreciable asset, borrowing to buy it may not always be a good idea. A bad debt is created when the borrower habitually takes out a loan to buy a vehicle. There has to be a point when it is no longer necessary to borrow in order to buy a personal vehicle. For this to be accomplished, the financial plan should be drawn up to also contain a savings program for the future purchase of a car. In a similar vein, taking out an excessive education loan—in the instance that the expected postcollege income cannot pay it off in a timely manner—may also be viewed as a case of bad debt.

Bad Debt—Consumer Loan

The worst forms of bad debt are payday loans and consumer loans, especially those held on a credit card. Bad debt buys things that depreciate as well as items that are disposable. Items that are disposable include clothing, household wares, food, and vacations.

To be clear, credit cards are useful because of the convenience they provide in making various online and telephone payments. They are also useful because often, they provide cash-back benefits and frequent flyer miles, and most importantly, they help boost one's credit score when used prudently. But for these benefits to be meaningful, the user must be prepared to pay the entire balance when due. It is a myth that owing on a credit card and then paying it off later is a good way to build credit. Credit card users do not need to owe beyond the allowed grace period to build up credit.

Using a credit card—a store or bank card—to make a purchase just because of a store promotion is unwise. It is unwise because the cardholder is buying something that is not really needed, except for the fact that it is offered at a discount. I remember an encounter with a certain young lady at one of my financial workshops in Northwest Indiana in 2010. She rightly described herself as a shopaholic. She made it a point to go shopping at her favorite department store every Tuesday because that store offered a 30 percent discount for all cardholders on that day. Eventually, she racked up so much personal debt on the store card that she was forced to file for personal bankruptcy.

One could argue that the moral of the story is that the store had it coming by extending credit to customers who were knowingly imprudent with their spending. However, considering the importance of maintaining a good credit, I think it is unwise to go shopping just because one has a bunch of discount coupons. This, I think, is a more helpful moral of the story. When funds are tight, it is wise to go shopping for only the items that are needed and can be afforded. And if there are discount coupons for those items, then so much the better.

Bad Debt—Stock Market Loan

Borrowing to *play* the stock market—as some are tempted to do—is like playing a game of Russian roulette and is very dangerous financially. Keep in mind that loans require fixed repayments to be made at fixed time intervals. Stocks, on the other hand, do not provide fixed incomes at fixed intervals. Dividends are not promised, and the stocks may not have increased in value when it is time to sell them to pay off the loan. This cash flow mismatch is the beginning of a dangerous game. If the stock market tanks when it is time to repay the loan, the borrower might not secure enough funds from the stock sale—a problem that could result in bankruptcy.

Paying Off Bad Debt

Bankruptcy should never be an option unless it is absolutely impossible to pay off personal debt. Bankruptcy not only worsens a person's credit score, but it also hurts a credit record for many years to come. As a result, the individual will be denied credit for several years into the future. It is also a common practice that many landlords and rental agencies do not rent to individuals with bad credit. Notwithstanding, bankruptcy may be the only lifeline when personal debt cannot be discharged in any other way. It is important, however, to be aware that education loans are not dischargeable in personal bankruptcy, as I have repeatedly mentioned in this book.

To pay off personal debt and begin to repair credit, a step-by-step approach is helpful. All outstanding debt balances should be arranged in a stack from the worst troubling at the top to the least troubling at the bottom. The debt balance at the top should be paid off first, followed by the next in line; the debt elimination should continue in that descending order.

At the top of the stack are the delinquent loans. These are the most serious if bankruptcy is to be avoided. Next in line are the high interest-bearing loans because of the high additional interest charges that accrue on the unpaid balance. The third level lists the so-called bad debts, which include outstanding credit card loans, other consumer loans, and overdue auto loans. Finally, at the bottom are the good debts, which are primarily overdue mortgage and outstanding student loans. Again, it is helpful to include debt payoff in the budget section of a financial plan as I have already demonstrated.

Sometimes the amounts owed may belong in the same category of debt, such as consumer credit. In such a case, it is helpful to place the smallest amount at the top of the debt pyramid and the largest at the bottom; meaning, the smallest debt is paid off first followed by the next smallest amount, in that order. Doing this improves personal credit and perhaps also, sense of comfort. It improves personal credit because each debt that is paid off, regardless of how small the amount may be, effectively reduces the number of creditors on one's credit record.

Building a Good Credit

When building a good credit is desired, it is not necessary to carry multiple credit cards. Also, it is not necessary to carry individual store credit cards. Bank credit cards with loyalty programs are preferable. Bank cards do the same job as store cards and also enable the cardholder to make various other payments for which store cards cannot be used. One or two low-cost bank cards are sufficient for building good credit. It is true that cancelling unwanted credit cards may hurt the cardholder's FICO (credit) score. Notwithstanding, it is prudent to balance this disadvantage with the temptation to go shopping at will and accumulate unnecessary debt.

Finally, it is helpful to view credit cards as *convenience cards*. In this sense, credit cards offer four key benefits to the cardholder: (1) they are safer to carry than cash; (2) they are convenient for making online payments; (3) they are useful for tracking and managing purchases and payments; and (4) the cardholder can earn loyalty rewards such as cash back, free hotel stays, and mileage credit. Outside of these four instances, it may not be wise to use credit cards, especially if the risk of carrying a balance beyond the grace period is high. A point never to ignore is that the financing cost on most credit cards far exceeds how much one can expect to earn on any financial market investment.

Financial prudence calls for one to be careful with spending and in particular, to keep spending within the bounds of disposable income. Underdeveloped nations are variously poor because they have yet to develop an efficient means of harnessing their resources to create wealth for their citizens. In the industrialized West, our perennial problem has been how the money we earn from the efficient utilization of our resources is spent. When money is spent unwisely, it creates financial hardship, sometimes leading to the same type of poverty that exists in the less developed economies. This is a contradiction in terms that, fortunately, is avoidable through careful financial planning.

PART III

A National Perspective

Chapter 8: Attacking Our Crippling National Debt

Avoiding likewise the accumulation of debt, not only by shunning occasions of expense, but by vigorous exertions in time of peace to discharge the debts which unavoidable wars have occasioned, not ungenerously throwing upon posterity the burden which we ourselves ought to bear.

—*George Washington*

The last three chapters looked at the dangers of excessive personal debt and the virtues of financial prudence. Incidentally, our personal struggles with money and debt, for the most part, mirror the financial state of the United States government, especially since 2000. Between 2011 and 2013, however, the economic story that dominated the world was the Eurozone Debt Crisis. Leading the pack of European countries on the brink of bankruptcy was Greece, whose public debt in 2011 was estimated at 164 percent of the country's gross domestic product (GDP).[44]

Greece's situation—or for that matter the situation of any of the other heavily indebted European countries—was, in fact, not so different from the fiscal picture of the United States at the time. On this side of the Atlantic, our debt-to-GDP ratio in 2012 exceeded 100 percent, meaning that how much we owed was larger than the size of our entire economy.

---

44 Costas Paris and Geoffrey T. Smith, "IMF Draft See Greek Debt Reaching 129% of GDP in 2020," *The Wall Street Journal Europe*, accessed February 19, 2012, http://online.wsj.com/article/SB10001424052970204131004577233491728095470.html.

This sad story sets the premise for the account and perspectives I share in this third and final part of this book.

The fiscal challenges confronting the United States in the first decade of the current millennium was a long time in the making. Many would agree that it was the result of excessive borrowing that could be easily traced back to the early 1980s. The Cold War with the Soviet Union rose to a tipping point in the early to mid-1980s when the United States spent heavily to build up its strategic weaponry. This was in response to the Soviet intermediate range ballistic missiles deployed in Eastern Europe at the time. Much of the money spent to build up our military was borrowed, as the United States had already entered into a long phase of fiscal deficits. The debt burden eased somewhat in the mid- to late 1990s, owing to the productivity gains from the high technology boom. However, the spending spree took a turn for the worse after the September 11, 2001, terror attacks. That event of infamy marked the beginning of the long and very expensive war on terrorism.

The financial bottom eventually fell out following the collapse of the housing market in 2007. All the money spent by the government in 2008 and 2009 to bail out Wall Street and stimulate the economy was borrowed. We did not have sufficient tax revenues to pay for the massive spending to rescue the economy.

The problem with our long-running spending spree is not necessarily what the money is spent on. The problem, as I see it, has more to do with our ideological divide on how best to grow the economy and create jobs. Some of us sincerely believe that the best approach is to cut taxes, reduce spending, and keep the government lean. Others believe as strongly that massive government spending plus tax cuts for the middle class are what is needed to fix the economy. Unfortunately, these old and tired ideological positions are often taken at the expense of the nation's financial security. These arguments fail to address how any fiscal deficits resulting from these positions would be handled should the economy lose steam.

We should accept the fact that governments, Democratic or Republican, will always spend money for a variety of purposes, even though we, as a people, might disagree on the spending priorities. However, in addition to debating how the money should be spent, should we not also ask where the money will come from? Will it be borrowed, or will it come from tax revenues? And if we plan to spend more than the projected tax revenues, whatever the reasons might be, how would the deficit be financed? By raising taxes or borrowing?

Politicians understand that if by borrowing they can grow the economy and create jobs, voters will be less inclined to worry about debt. That was exactly what happened in the 1980s, especially in the last five years of President Reagan's eight years in office. The economy grew rapidly. The unemployment rate fell from 11 percent earlier in his presidency to only 6 percent when he left office in January 1989. But underneath it all, our national debt grew by almost 160 percent from start to finish of Reagan's presidency.

Equally, it is possible to grow the economy and create jobs by massively increasing government spending with additional tax revenues. An example was in 1993 when one of the largest peace-time tax increases was signed into law by President Bill Clinton.[45] Many might recall that it took Vice President Al Gore, acting in his capacity as Senate President, to break the tie in the Senate and pass that tax bill. It was this legislation that raised income tax rates for individuals to a record 39.6 percent.[46]

With the remarkable economic growth, extensive job creation, and low inflation in the mid- to late 1990s, Clinton's reelection in 1996 was a shoo-in. For good measure, the country also enjoyed a couple of years of budget surpluses late in Clinton's second term, a feat that had not been achieved in more than three decades. When Clinton was about to leave office in December 1999, the unemployment rate was 4.2 percent, the lowest in thirty years. That said, it is also true that during Clinton's eight years in office, our national debt grew by 42 percent.

US public debt grew more rapidly in the years after Clinton left office. In addition, in 2004—and for the first time in history—the amount of US government debt held by foreign investors exceeded the amount held by US investors. Consider this, is it not ironic that while we tout ourselves

---

45 Deficit Reduction Act of 1993 (Omnibus Budget Reconciliation Act, 1993); "The Clinton Tax Bill," *The New York Times* (Archives), May 14, 1993, www.nytimes.com/1993/05/14/us/the-clinton-tax-bill-clinton-proposal-for-tax-increases-passes-first-test.html?pagewanted=all&src=pm.

46 There is a lively debate among pundits and economists as to whether—on an inflation-adjusted basis—the 1982 Deficit Reduction tax bill orchestrated by President Reagan and the GOP's Senator Dole was larger than President Clinton's 1993 tax bill.

as the world's only superpower, we nevertheless continue to rely on the good graces of foreign nationals to finance our national budget?

Just as is the case with personal debt, there comes a time when the side effects of excessive national debt become crippling. At such times, it is much more difficult to stimulate the economy using the familiar tax incentives or spending increases. In a 2011 study on the consequences of excessive public debt, three economists with the Bank for International Settlements (BIS) found that countries with a high debt-to-GDP ratio (of more than 85 percent) tend to grow at a much lower pace.[47] This evidence was confirmed by the weak to sluggish economic growth that character-ized the Bush and Obama administrations in the 2000s.

Back in the fall of 2011, when data for this book were being assem-bled, total US national debt was about $15 trillion, of which a third was money borrowed from foreign investors.[48] It grew to an estimated $17 trillion in the final quarter of 2013. I doubt that the sad story of our huge national debt will have changed markedly by the time anyone reads this book—particularly if the rhetoric on tax and spend, rather than debt reduction and growth, continues to dominate the fiscal conversation.

The debt situation in 2011 was a crisis trigger for three important reasons. First, and as has already been pointed out, this amount of debt was greater than our total economic output. Second, a significant por-tion of the debt was held by outsiders, mostly sovereign governments. Third, because the United States is the largest economy in the world, our weakness—economic or political—can have a far greater negative impact on the global stage than any European or Asian financial crisis ever could. The confidence the world places in the US economic and po-litical strength is the sole reason the vast majority of the world's tradable assets are dollar-denominated. It is also the reason that the largest foreign currency reserves held by almost every country are in US dollars.

Regardless of anyone's political persuasion or ideological leaning, the fact remains that the solution to our fiscal crisis would require pain and courage. Regrettably, some of us are sticking to the argument that we

---

47 Stephen G Cecchetti, M. S. Mohanty, and Fabrizio Zampolli, "The Real Effects of Debt," 2010, accessed on February 25, 2012, www.bis.org/publ/othp16.pdf.

48 "Ownership of Federal Securities," U.S. Department of the Treasury, Bureau of the Public Debt, March 2012.

can somehow fix this gargantuan debt problem and yet grow the economy sustainably using either tax incentives alone or more government spending. For those who think in this way, keep in mind that even before any meaningful attempt to tackle our national debt can be made, we first have to eliminate our annual budget deficits, which, in 2012 alone, was estimated at more than $1 trillion.[49]

Failed Attempts to Reduce Public Debt

I think it is fair to point out that the White House and Congress made a few meaningful attempts to resolve the debt crisis, especially after the fiscal mess that resulted from the 2008 financial crisis. What follows is a recap of the efforts and the failures.

On February 18, 2010, President Barack Obama empanelled the bipartisan National Commission on Fiscal Responsibility and Reform. The commission was co-chaired by Erskine Bowles and former Wyoming senator Alan Simpson. The commission's report, presented on December 3, 2010, recommended $4 trillion in savings over ten years. Unfortunately, their recommendation failed the committee stage, as it required a supermajority of fourteen out of eighteen votes to pass. Only eleven of eighteen votes were in favor. That bill also failed in the Senate when six of the senators who originally cosponsored the legislation joined others to vote against it.

In the early summer of 2011, House Speaker John Boehner and President Obama negotiated what was referred to as a "grand bargain." The deal would cut government spending by up to $3.5 trillion over ten years as well as increase tax revenues by a trillion dollars over the same period. On July 22, 2011, the deal fell apart even before it was brought to Congress for a vote.[50] To show its disappointment, the stock market plunged by four percentage points in the trading week that followed.

---

49 "Budget and Economic Outlook: Fiscal Years 2011 to 2021," Congressional Budget Office, report published on January 26, 2011, accessed May 3, 2012, www.cbo.gov/publication/21999.

50 One of several editorials on this issue appeared in the following article: "Obama's evolution: Behind the failed 'grand bargain' on the debt," *Washington Post*, accessed December 26, 2013, http://articles.washingtonpost.com/2012-03-17/politics/35447393_1_president-obama-eric-cantor-republicans.

Public criticisms on the failure by political leaders to reach an agreement led to a flurry of efforts in Congress to forge a compromise and avoid a national debt default. In the negotiations that followed, Congress tied raising the debt ceiling to a debt reduction agreement. By increasing the debt ceiling periodically, the US Treasury is able to borrow additional money with which to pay off maturing debt, make required interest payments on existing debt, and finance additional deficit spending. Unfortunately, the resulting legislation, which was passed on August 2, 2011 (the Budget Control Act of 2011), provided for only $1 trillion in long-term spending cuts and did not include any revenue increase.

Many were disappointed by this paltry effort to reduce our public debt. Also, the political drama and harsh rhetoric that preceded the passage of this legislation did much to harm investor confidence in the financial markets. To show its disapproval of the government's failure to come up with a meaningful debt reduction plan, the bond ratings company Standard & Poor's downgraded the US government's credit rating from AAA to AA+ on August 5, 2011. This was the first time in the history of the United States that the US Treasury's credit rating was downgraded. On the next trading day, the stock market tumbled by seven percentage points.

In response to the series of negative financial market reactions to the failed budget talks, Congress set up what it called a supercommittee of six Democrats and six Republicans. This committee was charged with finding ways to reduce the running deficits. Unfortunately, on November 21, 2011, the committee announced that it could not come to an agreement. Once again, the ideological divide on tax and spend stood in the way. One side argued that it was unfair to tax the rich in order to balance the national budget; after all, the rich were not to blame for our debt problem. Moreover, it would be unwise to raise taxes on anyone in a weak economy.

The other side argued it would be unfair to cut spending in a manner that would reduce benefits to seniors; after all, seniors worked hard and made their fair contribution to build up our economy. Additionally, as the argument went, it would be inequitable to focus on spending cuts rather than bring in more tax dollars from the wealthy since, based on the prevailing tax code, the average tax rate of the very rich was lower than that of the middle and lower income classes.

I think it is fair to say that each of these views has merit under all but the most unusual economic conditions. Fixing our recurring fiscal deficits and cutting the crushing national debt ought to be viewed apart from the beliefs that traditionally guide our political debates. The specific ways that fiscal decisions are made using taxation and spending ought not to be confused with the sacrifices that need to be made to halt the deepening debt crisis.

When debt outweighs income, a predicament similar to Shakespeare's Antonio versus Shylock in the *Merchant of Venice* is inevitable. In such an event, financial freedom lies at the mercy of the lender, who may not be quite so favorably disposed toward the borrower. I remember that following the downgrading of US credit rating in 2011, Secretary of State Hilary Clinton made a trip to Beijing to reassure the Chinese of the safety of their massive holdings of US Treasury securities.[51] In many ways, this awkward turn of events is a contradiction in terms—given that the American economic model is the basis for the growing wealth and strength of China in the twenty-first century.

Too Much Spending and Too Little Revenue

It is indeed true that our national debt problem is the result of excessive spending. This can be easily confirmed by noting that government spending grew from 18 to 25 percent of our gross domestic product (GDP) between 2000 and 2010. It is equally true that our budget deficits were made worse by reduced tax revenues. Federal budget data show that revenues, as a percent of GDP, fell from 21 percent in 2000 to less than 15 percent in 2010.[52] The math is simple, really. Spending more and taking in less will surely land the country deep in the hole.

Cutting spending is often an easier political argument to make. The reason might be that many of us believe that a significant portion

---

51 "China Worried about US Treasury Holdings," *USA Today*, accessed December 24, 2013, http://abcnews.go.com/Business/story?id=7084926.

52 Congressional Budget Office, "Revenues, Outlays, Deficits, Surpluses, and Debt Held by the Public, 1971 to 2010, as a Percentage of Gross Domestic Product," Budget and Economic Outlook: Historical Budget Data, Table E-1, January 2011, accessed September 15, 2011, www.cbo.gov/publication/21999.

of government spending goes to unproductive programs and projects. However, a quick glance at our national budgets over the years reveals that in most cases, discretionary items account for no more than 20 percent of total government spending. Discretionary items are those in which we have wiggle room as to how much to spend. Therefore, for a spending cut to be meaningful in the context of debt reduction, it must include all budget items except, of course, our debt repayment obligations.

Similarly, revenue increases cannot rely on taxing the rich alone. It is unfair to single out the rich as if they did wrong by working hard to become wealthy. When viewed broadly, taxing the rich differentially is un-American since most, if not all, of us aspire to also become financially self-sufficient through hard work.

For it to have some resonance, I believe the tax argument should be framed differently—strictly in the context of debt reduction. There might be two axes to pursue. First, if our tax system is unfair, then the discourse should focus solely on revising the tax code to make it fairer for everyone, regardless of income level. I think the appeal in the unsuccessful presidential bid of Herman Cain in 2011 was his proposed simple tax model of 9-9-9 (9 percent sales tax, 9 percent corporate tax, and 9 percent income tax). His plan would eliminate all deductions, which typically favor the very rich. The second approach might be to argue for an extraordinary taxation as a one-time remedy for the debt problem. I suppose that if taxes are levied with the specific goal of applying the incremental revenues to debt reduction, few might oppose it, especially if the urgency of the debt crisis is clear to all.

Using a special levy to eliminate debt is not unprecedented. Following the 1997-1998 Asian Financial Crisis, South Korea was forced to take out a $19.5 billion loan from the International Monetary Fund (IMF). Pressed by the stringent structural controls imposed by the IMF and other lenders, South Korean citizens accepted a special taxation. The high point was when Koreans went in droves to donate their gold and other jewelry to their national treasury. The result was a payoff of the country's bailout debt ten months ahead of schedule in August 2001.[53] Instead of the type of feel-good short-term monetary and fiscal fixes we are used to in the United States, Koreans saw the crisis as a national emergency, bit the bullet, and got the problem behind them.[54]

As unrealistic as it might be, it is quite possible that some of us truly believe that a debt of $15 trillion dollars (as of 2011) can be easily eliminated through reduced spending alone. It is challenging to see how this feat could be accomplished. Consider this: The one-year fiscal deficit in 2011 alone was a mind-boggling $1.3 trillion dollars. That is, we spent $1.3 trillion more than we collected in taxes. In that same year, 2011, the total spending was estimated at $3.4 trillion. Even if, theoretically, it were possible to spend absolutely nothing in the following fiscal year, we would only have been able to reduce our debt from $15 trillion to $11.6 trillion. Incidentally, $11.6 trillion was approximately the debt level in 2008 when the financial crisis erupted. At that time, our GDP was about $12 trillion. As can be easily seen, even such an impossible feat would do little to ease our debt burden. Likewise, it is naïve for anyone to think that the way out of the crisis is for the rich to pay more taxes. Even if we succeeded in doing this, the additional revenue that would be generated would do very little to reduce the national debt in any meaningful way.

Aligning Size of Debt with Size of Economy

At a community forum at the Purdue University campus in Hammond, Indiana, on September 15, 2011, I offered what I called a viable path to debt elimination. The first step is to set a long-term debt ceiling that cannot be exceeded. The ceiling itself is pegged to our nation's gross domestic product (GDP). I discovered that until the mortgage crisis of 2007, our average annual debt-to-GDP ratio was no more than about 60 percent,

---

53 The total loan from international financial organizations was $30.2 billion, including $19.5 billion from the IMF. "South Korea Pays of Debt to IMF," *People's Daily*, Friday, August 24, 2001, accessed February 18, 2012, http://english.people.com.cn/english/200108/24/eng20010824_78160.html.

54 "Lessons Learned, South Korea Makes Quick Economic Recovery," *The New York Times*, Asia Pacific, January 6, 2011, accessed February 18, 2012, www.nytimes.com/2011/01/07/world/asia/07seoul.html?_r=1.

meaning for every dollar we produced, we owed no more than sixty cents. This relationship largely held between 1980 and 2007.

Coincidentally, I also found that the average annual rate at which our economy grew—in nominal terms—during the same period was about 6 percent; sometimes it was more, sometimes it was less. Not being an economist, I was particularly struck by the fact that the 6 percent growth rate held for most extended periods of our economic history. Guided by this evidence, I concluded that the maximum debt-to-GDP ratio that would still allow for a normal economic growth is 60 percent.[55]

The second step was to determine how much and how long it would take us to reach the 60 percent debt/GDP goal. Because the process for making this determination would likely be politically contentious, I suggested it would be wise to delegate the task to a nonpartisan taskforce of experts rather than politicians. Once the timing and the required total savings are determined, the final step will be to look at the annual budgets and then work out how much spending to cut and how much extra revenue to bring in so as to have the required savings within the set period.

For this approach to have meaning, it might be important to consider the nature of the two aspects of federal spending in the budget. One aspect deals with *discretionary* items, which, as explained earlier, are those that can be easily revised up or down. Examples are education, infrastructure, and military. The other aspect of the budget deals with items that are pretty much etched in stone in the sense that they are fixed by law. Examples of these so-called *mandatory* items are Social Security and Medicare. Going forward, the percentage of each of these items in the budget would then be applied to reduce spending for that particular item over the debt correction period. I call this the pizza slice model.

To explain, suppose the total budget in a typical year is $100, of which military spending is $20 (which comes out to be 20 percent of the total). Now, suppose the savings goal is to reduce total spending in the

---

55 Data source for US GDP: Bureau of Economic Analysis, "National Income and Product Accounts: Gross Domestic Product," accessed May 20, 2014, www.bea.gov/national/index.htm#gdp.

Data source for US public debt: U.S. Department of the Treasury, "Monthly Statement of the Public Debt of the United States," Accessed May 20, 2014, www.treasurydirect.gov/govt/reports/pd/mspd/mspd.htm.

budget from $100 to $90. This would result in savings of $10. With this approach, the portion of the cut that will come from the military would also be 20 percent (of $10) or $2. The respective proportion of each of the other discretionary items would be applied in the same way to reduce spending for those items.

Using the pizza analogy, suppose you typically eat two slices of pizza from a pie of ten pieces; your share is 20 percent of the total pie. For reasons of austerity, a new order of pizza is downsized to only eight pieces. In keeping with your proportionate share, you would still be entitled to 20 percent of the total number of slices, which is now 1.6 slices—that is, 20 percent of eight pieces.

The mandatory items are trickier to handle, though, because the amounts are specified either by legislation or a previous commitment. For this reason, they must be negotiated but done so in a manner that ultimately adjusts them with respect to their proportionate share in the budget. While it is true that we have an obligation to meet these so-called unfunded mandates, we must also recognize that we cannot give what we do not have. Seniors, like everyone else, can be expected to share in the pain of fixing our debt problem since *all* of us have played a role in creating it.

For some budget items, there might be a threshold below which further cuts would be unrealistic. One way to deal with this constraint is to set lower limits for such items in the budget negotiations—without, of course, changing the savings goal.

The key benefit of this debt correction approach can be summarized as follows: by pegging the country's debt to the maximum level that can be sustained—based on the size of the economy—it helps to resolve the fiscal crisis in an unbiased and arguably, equitable manner. Nevertheless, it is not offered as an absolute reconciliation model but rather as a prudent approach to ultimately meet the desired fiscal goal of bringing down our national debt.[56]

Looking at our national debt with respect to economic growth offers an opportunity to ensure we have not borrowed beyond our means. In

---

56 The reference for the published study is as follows: Pat Obi and Raida Abuizam, "A Heuristic and Goal Programming Framework for Resolving the US Debt Crisis," *Journal of Current Research in Global Business*, Vol. 17, No. 27, 2014; pp. 1-12.

this way, political leaders are held to account regardless of which approach—tax reduction or increased spending—they use to stimulate the economy.

I believe that when in crisis, the common good should supersede the ideologies that shape partisan politics. It is true that espousing party-based ideologies that appeal to the local constituency helps get one elected into public office. I recall that Tip O'Neal, who was the House Speaker in the 1980s, is credited to have said that "all politics is local." However, while the local constituency might be delighted by partisan ideologies, the country's economic strength and global leadership may be compromised. Perhaps for this singular reason, term limits in Congress might not be a bad idea, as they would limit local constituency bias when voting on an important national issue.

As a final note, our country's economic problems are not all resolved when the economy grows and the unemployment rate drops. The grave error we make all too often is never questioning how economic growth is financed. Growth financed with borrowed money leaves us at the mercy of our lenders, who someday will come knocking at the door. This truth is even more compelling when a significant portion of our borrowed money comes from non-Americans.

In this era of globalization and intense international competition, we cannot expect to create a strong and sustainable economy with trillions of debt from abroad. Ultimately, we must be willing to live within our means, by either pegging our spending to the size of our economy or simply paying more taxes to fully finance our fiscal priorities. As the 2011 Eurozone debt crisis has revealed, excessive debt is never a sustainable path to building the wealth of any nation.

Chapter 9. Lessons from the 2008 Financial Crisis

Credit buying is much like being drunk. The buzz happens immediately and gives you a lift. The hangover comes the day after.

—*Joyce Brothers*

In the United States, as well as in many other parts of the world, we experienced an extraordinary run-up in home prices between 1990 and 2007. The housing boom was particularly dramatic in the six-year period ending in 2007. During that period, home prices rose by a record 60 percent. In comparison, home prices rose by only 20 percent in the preceding six-year period and, even then, it was unprecedented. At the height of the housing boom in March 2007, the average price for a single family home in the United States was $329,400, compared to only $171,000 a decade earlier.[57]

Few of us questioned how that housing boom was financed until the bubble burst in 2007. A lot of borrowed money—lots of it—poured into the housing market. Total household borrowing at the inception of the crisis in 2007 was a mind-boggling $1.2 trillion. It was only $310 billion ten years earlier. The result of all that borrowing was an escalation in household debt, which rose from $5.5 trillion in 1997 to $14 trillion in 2007. More than three quarters of that debt was invested in the housing

---

57 United States Census Bureau, "Median and Average Sales Prices of New Homes Sold in United States," U.S. Department of Commerce, accessed July 15, 2014, www.census.gov/const/uspricemon.pdf

market, which helped fuel the housing boom.[58] Ironically, the Federal Reserve reported that household wealth of $13 trillion was wiped out between 2007 and 2008, owing to the housing market collapse.[59] Certainly, this amount could not have been real wealth, since it was created out of grossly overvalued real estate investments.

After the collapse of the housing market in 2007 and the financial crisis that followed in 2008, many were quick to blame the Federal Reserve and Wall Street banks. The anti-Wall Street sentiments came to a head in the final months of 2011 with the Occupy Wall Street rallies around the country. I must confess that I felt the anti-Wall-Street campaigns might have been disingenuous. While Wall Street certainly played a significant role in the crisis, no one seemed to complain, back in the 1990s and 2000s, when the government and financial institutions made it very easy for us to borrow and buy homes that, in many cases, we could not afford.

True, there were many instances of predatory—and perhaps even deceptive—lending by many loan officers. Also, the so-called "originate-to-distribute" loan model, in which loan officers were more concerned with the size of the loans they made (due to higher commissions) rather than the quality of the loans, contributed greatly to the crisis. Through this conduct, loan officers ignored the risk of borrower default since their commissions were based on the volume of loans they made. As a result, the borrower's ability to repay the loan took a backseat.

It is also difficult to forget the careless and unregulated use of

---

58 Household borrowing: Federal Reserve Statistical Release, "Credit Market Borrowing by Sector," Financial Accounts of the United States, release date: March 6, 2014, accessed May 21, 2014, www.federalreserve.gov/releases/z1/current/accessible/d2.htm.

Household debt: Federal Reserve, "Credit Market Debt Outstanding by Sector," Federal Reserve, Flow of Funds Accounts, accessed December 24, 2013, www.federalreserve.gov/releases/z1/current/accessible/d3.htm. Household debt includes mortgage loans and consumer credit.

59 Barry P. Bosworth and Rosanna Smart, "The Wealth of Older Americans and the Subprime Debacle," Center for Retirement Research at Boston College, Working Paper 2009-21, November 2009. Also available online (accessed May 21, 2014) www.brookings.edu/research/papers/2009/11/18-wealth-bosworth.

difficult-to-understand financial products like collateralized debt obligations (CDOs) and credit default swaps (CDS). These so-called *derivatives*, which flooded the housing market with money from all over the world, gave speculators unfettered room to gamble on the likelihood that homeowners would default on their loans.

I think it is also fair to point out that Wall Street banks suffered greatly from the grave errors they made. Some of the big-name banks that either failed or collapsed at the peak of the crisis include Bear Stearns, IndyMac, Fannie Mae, Freddie Mac, Lehman Brothers, Merrill Lynch, AIG, Washington Mutual, and Wachovia. It is important to bear in mind that "Wall Street" is not a phantom. These failed financial institutions were owned by millions of Americans who risked their capital in pursuit of the American dream. Many of the investors who lost money are everyday people like you and me. They invested in the stocks of these corporations as part of their retirement and education savings. Without the kind of investments these individuals make, there would be no employment for millions of Americans. For every firm that failed, many lost their investments, and many more lost their jobs.

Equally important, we should not be so quick to blame the Obama administration and the John Boehner's 112th Congress for the wrecked economy they inherited in 2009. The creation of easy money that enticed millions into the housing market began well before their time in high office. The unregulated trading of those credit derivatives was enabled by the Commodity Futures Modernization Act of 2000. Neither President Obama nor Speaker Boehner was in their respective offices at the time.

The availability of subprime mortgage loans gained momentum from the mid-1990s, when both Fannie Mae and Freddie Mac were urged by Congress to expand their portfolio of mortgages to include high risk mortgage-backed securities. These high-risk securities provided funds for subprime loans. Three key regulations in the 1990s steered us in this direction. In 1992, the Federal Housing Enterprises Financial Safety and Soundness Act required Fannie Mae and Freddie Mac to devote a percentage of their lending to support "affordable housing," code for subprime loans. In 1993, the Federal Reserve Bank of Boston published "Closing the Gap: A Guide to Equal Opportunity Lending," which recommended a series of measures to provide greater access to credit for low-income households. Finally, the Community Reinvestment Act of

1995 created the basis to break down home loan data by neighborhood, income, and race. This last legislation made it possible for Fannie Mae to receive "affordable housing credit" for providing funds for subprime loans.

While these regulations were well intentioned, the massive default of subprime loans that triggered the mortgage crisis ultimately led to the collapse of Fannie Mae and Freddie Mac in 2008. The US government was forced to take over these financial institutions since, by law, the loans they sold were backed by the full faith and credit of the federal government (translation: tax payers). Therefore, we should not be quick to blame Fannie and Freddie for something we all wanted, and something that was facilitated by various acts of Congress.

One of the modern economists I greatly admire is Alan Greenspan, Chairman of the US Federal Reserve Board of Governors from 1987 to 2006. We cannot forget the admirable leadership he showed during the market crash of October 19, 1987 (Black Monday), the recession of the early 1990s, and, most importantly, the September 11, 2001 terror attacks. Some have blamed him for contributing to the 2008 financial crisis by keeping interest rates too low and not warning us of the looming danger. I did not think this criticism was well-founded.

Most observers know full well that the Federal Reserve's monetary policy is primarily guided by the mandate to grow the economy, keep inflation low, and make it easy for businesses to hire. If maintaining low interest rates is the way to accomplish these goals, the Fed would do just that. That was exactly what the Fed did, especially in the years after the bursting of the dot-com bubble (in 1999–2000) and the recession that followed. Many of us were quite impressed by the masterful way with which Greenspan wrested the economy from the brink. Overall, my opinion is that he did a stellar job during his term as chairman of the Federal Reserve System (he remains on my website as one of my most admired persons of all time).

Notwithstanding, Greenspan might have overlooked an important aspect of the crisis that few have identified. In his book *The Age of Turbulence*, he touts the widespread home ownership in the 2000s, noting that nearly 69 percent of American households owned their own homes–up from 44 percent in 1940. He also noted that low-income Americans, mostly blacks and Hispanics, were the greatest beneficiaries because of the government's support for subprime mortgage programs. His view that this expansion of homeownership boded well for the future of the country, I think, ignored the danger inherent in loans with high default risk. This view of credit risk was also set aside by another notable economist, Robert Samuelson, who in his writing in *Newsweek* on December 30, 2002, noted that the housing boom saved the US economy.

In my own self-examination, I have come to the conclusion, albeit with great difficulty, the we, in the American household, were perhaps the chief culprits of the mortgage crisis. We bought and flipped properties like they were going out of style. We took out huge mortgage loans even when we knew we did not have the income to support the loan payments. Many of us provided false income and asset information on the loan applications, knowing that little or no due diligence would be conducted by the lender. Aflush with a lot of cash, we proceeded to buy homes that were beyond our means, knowing full well that we were in over our heads. And, for good measure, we took out incalculable amounts of second mortgages to add more structures to our already large homes, purchase more automobiles, go on vacations, and flip more homes in a bid to rake in huge gains. No one held us at ransom to sign those loan applications.

If we claim to be victims of predatory lending, then we are in effect saying that we were incapable of making sound financial judgments for ourselves. Lest I am misunderstood, those predatory lenders should never be excused for what they did wrong. They preyed on seniors and others who had little knowledge of the mortgage markets and egged them on to take out adjustable rate mortgages with little or no down payments. These loans were later repriced at much higher interest rates. One of the sordid stories was revealed in late 2011 when Bank of America agreed to a settlement with the US Justice Department for unfair lending practices. The settlement required Bank of America to pay $335 million to resolve allegations that its Countrywide Home Loan unit engaged in a widespread pattern of discrimination against black and Hispanic borrowers.[60]

All that said, we should accept primary responsibility for the financial choices we make. I suppose it would be naïve to assume that every one of us was hoodwinked into borrowing more than we could afford. Placing all the blame on the loan officer or Wall Street or the government for our misuse of funds is like laying all the blame of a drug problem on the drug dealer. I do not think the dealer would be in business without the consumer. I believe it is healthy to take initial responsibility for our follies—even when others may have truly contributed to the problem. As the old adage says, if something seems too good to be true, it probably is. This is a lesson from which we could all benefit whenever we are tempted into any financial transactions that look exceedingly, or abnormally, attractive.

It is clear that excessive debt by homeowners was ultimately what triggered the mortgage crisis. We borrowed without much regard to our financial capacity. Here are two key questions that might help place this viewpoint in proper perspective: If homeowners had sufficient income to service their debt, would there have been the widespread defaults that gave rise to the wave of home foreclosures at the time? And without the massive delinquencies in 2007, would there really have been a financial crisis in 2008? Without enough income to service debt, we lay the groundwork for a financial disaster, especially in cases where the equity portion of home value is next to zero—as was the case with most, if not all, of the subprime loans at that time.[61]

---

60 Department of Justice, "Justice Department Reaches $335 Million Settlement to Resolve Allegations of Lending Discrimination by Countrywide Financial Corporation," Department of Justice Office of Public Affairs, Wednesday, December 21, 2011, accessed May 21, 2014, www.justice.gov/opa/pr/2011/December/11-ag-1694.html. It was determined that Countrywide Financial Corporation, prior to its 2008 acquisition by Bank of America, charged more than 200,000 African-American and Hispanic borrowers higher fees and interest rates than non-Hispanic white borrowers with similar credit.

61 In their National Delinquency Survey on December 6, 2007, the US Mortgage Bankers Association reported that while 13 percent of loans outstanding were subprime, more than half of home foreclosures at that time were subprime mortgage loans.

Sadly, when laws are made to encourage easy credit that leads to financial crisis, the taxpayer is ultimately liable. Consider the overall liability to the US taxpayer on account of the crisis. First, there was the Economic Stimulus Act of 2008, signed into law on February 13, 2008, by President George W. Bush. This legislation gave away more than $152 billion in tax rebate checks. President Bush called it a "booster shot." Second, there was the $700 billion Wall Street bailout (Emergency Economic Stabilization Act of 2008) which the then Treasury Secretary Henry Paulson championed. President George W. Bush signed this bill into law on September 28, 2008. Finally, there was the contentious $787 billion economic stimulus bill signed into law by President Barack Obama on February 17, 2009. The overall tally of the entire fiscal stimulus was a tidy $1.6 trillion.

As it turned out, all of this money was borrowed by the federal government, since our budget was already in the red. There should therefore be little wonder that our national debt ballooned to more than 100 percent of our gross domestic product by the end of 2011. This is a road we should never walk again, for as Publilius Syrus put it in ancient times, "debt is the slavery of the free."

Chapter 10. Final Thoughts

For we must consider that we shall be as a city upon a hill. The eyes of all people are upon us.

—*John Winthrop*

At the outset of this book, I shared my reflections of what I consider the three pillars of the American dream: educational excellence, hard work, and financial prudence. Through the years, I have discovered these to be the values that have particularly shaped the American nation in ways that few countries have experienced. By embracing them, we built a vibrant economic system that enabled us to be the most advanced and productive nation in the modern world. We also, for good measure, developed the type of innovative learning environment in our universities that continues to attract and educate millions from all over the world.

Through our efforts to innovate and lead, we kept the notion of "American exceptionalism" alive, which is a term often used to describe how qualitatively different we are in our cultural, political, and economic choices. In this respect, our nation has opened the door of opportunities to millions of Americans, making the realization of the often-talked-about American dream possible.

There is an unselfish element to the pursuit of the American dream that I find even more compelling. It is the deep sense of generosity of the American people. Such acts of exceptional kindness are particularly evident in turbulent times, such as when natural disasters and acts of terror occur. Besides helping one another during such times, we are also quick to reach out to the less fortunate in the far-flung parts of the world. A survey conducted by Charities Aid Foundation in 2011 showed that Americans ranked at the top when it comes to donations to charity, volunteer work, and willingness to help out a stranger.[62] This same spirit of generosity is also seen in our willingness to forgive and overlook the missteps of our public figures and others with fame and fortune.

In the workplace, Americans are known to be exceptionally hard-working, putting in more work hours per year than is the case in any other country. The American worker is well-known for demonstrating a work ethic that is second to none. Also, professionalism and fine workmanship are well entrenched in American industry. The challenge in the current times, however, is how to best prepare tomorrow's workforce not only to meet the higher demands of new industries but to also successfully compete internationally while seeking to attain a standard of living that is not reliant on debt.

To maintain the gains we have made over the years, we must be quick to upgrade our competencies. Without the type of basic education capable of providing the capacities to compete and excel internationally, our global leadership and economic strength may become impossible to sustain. And, in that regard, any suggestion that our best days are behind us may begin to gain traction. As a global leader, our performance gauge should stretch beyond the bounds of the United States. To be solely inward-looking, as some of us tend to be, is to deny ourselves the benefit of knowing the speed at which others are running the same race.

Global leadership goes hand in hand with economic strength, which—unfortunately—cannot be sustained with excessive debt and political grandstanding. The fiscal crisis that came to a head in 2011 and again in 2013 was gravely worrisome to many Americans. The idea of continuing to finance our budget with increasingly borrowed funds, especially from countries that are not so friendly to us, is hard to imagine. Equally unimaginable is the notion that some of our political leaders would prefer a government shutdown and the embarrassment of a debt default as the means to make a political point.

---

62 Charities Aid Foundation is a UK-based nonprofit organization advocating charitable giving. Its survey (World Giving Index) was based on 150,000 interviews with citizens of 153 countries. Survey results reported by The Christian Science Monitor, "Americans are the Most Generous, Global Poll Finds," December 21, 2011, www.cs-monitor.com/World/Making-a-difference/Change-Agent/2011/1221/Americans-are-the-most-generous-global-poll-finds.

At the individual level, the amassing of personal assets with mostly borrowed money may not be so bad if the value of those assets exceeded the amount of the loan. Sadly, for many of us, our household debt—created mostly from mortgage and consumer loans—far exceeds the value of the assets that were purchased with the loan. It is easy to see that as our personal and public debts have grown through the years, so have the financial difficulties in our households, a condition that for many of us has undermined the realization of the American dream.

Throughout this book, I have steadfastly maintained that to avoid the legacy of crushing debt, we must learn to consume less than we earn—a cliché that seems almost too mundane to be weighty. Yet, it is by embracing a prudent approach to managing money—both at the individual and national levels—that we can create lasting wealth as well as peace of mind.

Living beyond our means was not always part of the American story—at least not until the turn of the twenty-first century. As the calendar flipped to the new millennium, home prices rose steadily to unsustainable highs and then quickly crashed in 2007. The extensive use of high risk, unaffordable loans to purchase properties at that time fueled the financial crisis that eventually plunged the country—and, indeed, the world—into the Great Recession that began in 2009. If, because of that financial crisis, we have become smarter with our money, then perhaps there was a silver lining in it after all.

The stakes associated with financial prudence and good education have never been higher. The data presented in this book show quite clearly that it is much more difficult to get a job and earn a living wage for individuals without a college education. Unfortunately, many of our public grammar schools are ill-equipped to prepare students for the type of advanced learning that can enable them to compete successfully in the future. The failure of these schools, mostly in the inner cities, has several aspects to it, as I have outlined in this book. Many of these were depicted in the ABC *Nightline* presentation on May 31, 2013, in which Strawberry Mansion High School in Philadelphia was profiled. The problem that struck me particularly was not the unruly behavior of the students but rather the lack of involvement of the parents in their children's education. Without parental involvement, it was obvious that the best efforts of Principal Linda Wayman and her fine staff were insufficient to keep the students in check.

Given the unique set of challenges in many of our public schools, I have advanced an argument in favor of an education model in the style of a military academy. With this approach, students are provided with year-round boarding and holistic mentoring until they graduate. When a disciplined and controlled learning environment is in place, we are more assured of producing the right kind of students for our universities and ultimately, the workforce.

A good education also lays the foundation for not only what we can do to improve our personal lives but also what we can do for the benefit of others. The notion of changing the way we live, as articulated in this book, is one that begins with the acceptance of our individual responsibilities to work hard and strive to succeed in worthy endeavors and, as a result, become role models to others.

Personal success tends to have a contagion effect, in that others find reason to follow along the same line. Moreover, when a good education is combined with financial prudence, we stand on a firmer ground to not only enjoy a higher standard of living but also meaningfully contribute to the advancement of others. In my view, the litmus test of personal success is when one has the additional capability to make a lasting positive impact in the lives of others.

I believe that being mindful of our greater duty to society is ennobling; often, legacies are built in this manner. The flip side to this is living with an attitude of entitlement. This latter mindset has the tendency to cause us to set aside personal responsibilities and blame others for all our pitfalls. Such thinking is dangerous, especially because of the belief that society owes us everything with nothing to spare.

To be part of the great American story, I believe that a healthy ambition to nurture is to aspire to someday be a contributing member of society, and to accept the primary responsibility for our personal and professional development. While accepting the wisdom of this point of view, some of us are quick to add, however, that the absence of positive role models in many American homes has made this an unattainable reality for many young people, especially in the inner cities. This is true. But should we then throw in the towel and allow our youth to waste away?

Or, should we instead redouble our efforts to mentor and challenge the youth to work even harder, realizing that the alternative is not acceptable?

In my own American journey, I have been immensely fortunate to be the beneficiary of the generosity of many individuals. Even more significantly, I found it a treasured privilege in the few moments I proved useful to others, however meager the effort. This, to me, is the fulfillment of my American dream—the capacity to be valuable to others. The untold story of this great nation is how, by being good neighbors to others, we are able to mentor millions into lives that are no less successful than ours. This is the aspect of America that I find most inspiring.

By and large, the most enduring things done in life are those done for the benefit of society. The testament of many American greats—from Abraham Lincoln to Martin Luther King, Jr., and thousands more—is viewed in this light. Maya Angelou, the great American poet, once said in an episode of the *Oprah Winfrey Show*, sometime in the 1990s, that any person who is not useful beyond himself or herself is useless to society. I see no greater truth than this. Yet, regardless of our best intentions, we cannot make the type of effort that can prove useful to others unless we first equip ourselves with the capacity to do so. It is for this reason that the eternal benefits of a good education, hard work, and financial prudence can never be minimized.

Made in the USA
Lexington, KY
10 February 2019